THE
DIVINE
PLAN

THE DIVINE PLAN

John Paul II, Ronald Reagan, and
the Dramatic End of the Cold War

PAUL KENGOR

AND

ROBERT ORLANDO

ISI
BOOKS
WILMINGTON, DE

Cataloging-in-Publication Data is on file with the Library of Congress.

ISBN: 978-1-61017-154-0

Published in the United States by

ISI Books
Intercollegiate Studies Institute
3901 Centerville Road
Wilmington, DE 19807-1938
www.isibooks.org

Manufactured in the United States of America

"I've always believed that this blessed land was set apart in a special way, that some divine plan placed this great continent here between the two oceans to be found by people from every corner of the Earth—people who had a special love for freedom."
—*President Ronald Reagan, January 31, 1983*

"The only true freedom, the only freedom that can truly satisfy, is the freedom to do what we ought as human beings created by God according to his plan."
—*Pope John Paul II, September 10, 1987*

CONTENTS

PROLOGUE

TWO ACTORS IN
A DIVINE PLAN

S cene 1: Washington Hilton, March 30, 1981, 2:27 P.M.
President Ronald Reagan has just completed a speech before the AFL-CIO in Washington, D.C.

A crowd gathers outside the hotel to catch a glimpse of the president before he climbs into his motorcade. One young man in the crowd, John Hinckley, has other ideas. The deranged Hinckley has decided to make a dramatic bid for the attention of a Hollywood actress named Jodie Foster, his obsession.

Reagan hears what sounds like firecrackers. Suddenly, amid screams, Secret Service agent Jerry Parr shoves Reagan into the back seat of the presidential limousine. Parr lands on top of the president. "Jerry, get off," Reagan says. "I think you've broken one of my ribs."[1]

But the pain does not come from Parr. It comes instead from a razor-sharp bullet that has sliced near Reagan's heart—a bullet Hinckley had fired from his revolver.

At Parr's command, the driver abandons the plan to return to the White House and whisks Reagan to George Washington University Hospital. The president is bleeding severely.

Ronald Reagan is in mortal danger.

Scene 2: Saint Peter's Square, Vatican City, May 13, 1981, the feast day of Our Lady of Fátima, just past 5 p.m.

Only six weeks after the shooting of President Reagan, Pope John Paul II is riding in a small, white, open-air Fiat, better known as the Popemobile, greeting the thousands who have come to cheer him.

One man in the crowd has been waiting all day for his chance. Mehmet Ali Agca of Turkey carries a Browning 9-millimeter semiautomatic handgun.

As the pontiff draws close, Agca lifts the gun and fires four times. He hits the pope in the hand and in the abdomen. John Paul II collapses into the arms of his aides.

Father Stanisław Dziwisz, his close assistant and fellow Pole, asks the pope where he has been hit.

"In the stomach," the pope replies.

"Does it hurt?"

"It does."[2]

Agca begins running. But Sister Letizia, a tough Franciscan nun from Italy's Bergamo region, grabs him. Little does Agca know, but the sturdy nun pinning him down is saving his life. His Communist "friends" who planned the attack expect to greet him in the getaway truck with a bullet. They are not about to let their hired lackey live with this secret—or their cash. (As the historian Craig Shirley observes, "First rule of political assassination is to kill the assassin.")

Meanwhile, security officials get the pope into an ambulance and rush him to Gemelli Hospital. Rome's brutal traffic makes the task almost impossible, but the ambulance finally reaches the hospital, with only minutes to spare. When the patient arrives, doctors find that he is bleeding severely. His blood pressure is plummeting.

Father Dziwisz administers last rites.[3]

John Paul II is dying.[4]

Agca and his Bulgarian and Soviet handlers have set out to kill the pope.

But the Divine Plan has something else in store.

Kinship

A Catholic pope from Poland. A Protestant president from America's heartland.

A priest and philosopher. A Hollywood star and politician.

At first glance, Pope John Paul II and President Ronald Reagan seem to have little in common.

But look closer.

A careful examination of the pope and the president reveals many parallels. Some of these parallels, as we will see, involve biographical details. For example, their mothers both experienced major health crises when the boys were eight years old; their fathers died just two months apart in 1941; they both took unconventional paths to their positions of prominence.

The similarities run deeper, however. John Paul II and Reagan displayed a spiritual kinship that drew them to each other.

That kinship began with a shared understanding of the reinforcing relationship between faith and freedom. It comes as no surprise that the pope held this view. But this perspective animated Reagan as well. He did not take a narrow view of freedom as meaning merely "leave me alone." As president, he spoke of the "twin beacons of faith and freedom" and said that "freedom cannot exist alone" without faith.

Yes, Ronald Reagan was a man of faith—a point many biographers have underestimated. It was God, Reagan maintained, "from whom all knowledge springs."[5] The president told a group of students in 1983, "When we open ourselves to Him, we gain not only moral courage but also intellectual strength."[6]

John Paul II certainly agreed with Reagan on that point.

The president declared (quoting Father Theodore Hesburgh

of the University of Notre Dame), "Every person is a *res sacra*, a sacred reality."[7] Meanwhile, the pope said, "Every human being [is] somebody unique and unrepeatable."[8]

And both men identified the same paramount threat to faith, freedom, and human dignity: atheistic Communism. They saw Soviet Communism as a source of evil in the world—indeed, the great evil of the twentieth century.

Evil is not too strong a word to characterize the pope and the president's view of Communism. President Reagan famously referred to the Soviet Union as an "Evil Empire." John Paul II used similar language. In Poland, he suffered under two forms of totalitarianism—Nazism and then Communism. A decade before he became pope, he wrote of "atheistic ideologies" that represented "the evil of our times," because they resulted in a "degradation, indeed in a pulverization, of the fundamental uniqueness of each human person."

Reagan certainly agreed with John Paul II on that point.

Of all the parallels between Ronald Reagan and John Paul II, the most striking involves their respective attempted assassinations. Just six weeks apart in the spring of 1981, the president and the pope took bullets from would-be assassins.

At the time, few realized how close both men came to dying. John Hinckley's bullet missed Reagan's heart by mere centimeters, while Mehmet Ali Agca's barely missed John Paul II's main abdominal artery.[9] Had the bullets reached those targets, both Reagan and the pope probably would have bled to death before they reached the hospital.[10]

These near-death experiences—this shared suffering—forged a singular bond between the pope and the president, one that historians have failed to appreciate.

Even before the shootings, John Paul II and Reagan had sensed their philosophical kinship. Before he ever became president, Reagan had identified the pope as an essential ally, someone who shared his principled aversion to Communism and could help rescue the millions trapped behind the Iron Curtain. In the words of his first national security adviser, Richard V. Allen, "Reagan had a deep and steadfast conviction that this pope would help change the world."[11]

But it was the assassination attempts that really brought them together. They began a rich correspondence, and when they met for the first time in the Vatican a year after the shootings, they confided to each other a shared conviction: that God had spared their lives for a reason.

That reason? To defeat Communism.

In private, Reagan had a name for this: "The DP"—the Divine Plan.

"THE DESIGNS OF PROVIDENCE"

While historians have underestimated the depth and importance of the bond between John Paul II and Ronald Reagan, they have also failed to explore the notion of a Divine Plan.

Now, isn't that to be expected? The story of the end of the Cold War is dramatic enough without bringing in questions about a divine hand in human affairs. Why even bother raising such questions?

The answer is: *because both John Paul II and Reagan firmly believed in the Divine Plan and felt sure that they had been called to play their roles in it.*

The Divine Plan drove both the pope and the president.

This is not speculation. Reagan spoke of "The DP" often, with family, friends, and aides. He and William P. Clark, his closest adviser dating back to the 1960s, with whom he frequently prayed, discussed God's hand in events so often that the DP shorthand became a staple of their conversations. And as we will see, Reagan didn't hesitate to discuss his belief in Divine Providence publicly, including in speeches and in his memoirs. When a striking series of apparent coincidences occurred, Reagan looked to a heavenly hand for an explanation.

So did John Paul II. The pope became famous for saying, "In the designs of Providence there are no mere coincidences." He also declared that "the destiny of all nations lies in the hands of a merciful Providence."

You can't understand Pope John Paul II and President Ronald Reagan without understanding how much faith they put in the Divine Plan.

Nor can you understand how the Cold War came to such a swift and peaceful end without understanding their conviction that the Divine Plan had assigned them roles to help improve the lives of millions suffering under Communism.

Taking the World Stage

> *All the world's a stage,*
> *And all the men and women merely players;*
> *They have their exits and their entrances,*
> *And one man in his time plays many parts.*
>   —Shakespeare, *As You Like It*, Act 2, Scene 7

The parts John Paul II and Reagan played in the drama of the end of the Cold War became the roles of their lives.

But like all of us, they had played many other parts in their time.

Shakespeare's metaphor of the stage applies particularly well to the pope and the president. Among the many parallels between their lives, an especially intriguing one is the fact that both were actors before they took the world stage. Reagan, of course, enjoyed a lengthy career in Hollywood and then as the host of one of television's most popular programs. But a young Karol Wojtyła—the man who became Pope John Paul II—also had extensive acting experience. In fact, his ambition as a young man was to become an actor. He later wrote that in high school his "vocation to the priesthood had not yet matured," because he was "completely absorbed by a passion for literature, especially dramatic literature, and for the theater."[12] He threw himself into stage acting and wrote six plays as well.

For this book we conducted exclusive interviews with more than a dozen authorities on John Paul II and Reagan—historians, biographers, and close advisers. Virtually all of them commented on the acting experience the pope and the president had in common. This experience may seem like little more than a curiosity, but as we will see, their acting skills became crucial to their later success as leaders.

For example, presidential historian Douglas Brinkley, editor of *The Reagan Diaries*, suggests that acting helped John Paul II and Reagan become extraordinary communicators. And communication "is the number-one attribute of a leader," Brinkley says. "In the end, you can't do anything or get very far if you don't have the skills to communicate." As actors, John Paul II and Reagan learned how to command audiences.

It is easy to think of acting as *faking*, as fooling audiences into believing something untrue. But the pope and the president excelled at communicating core convictions—"the principles and values by which they stood," as the historian Stephen Kotkin puts it. They learned to convey—to act out—their deepest beliefs in simple words that moved people and nations to action.

This is no coincidence, certainly not in the case of John Paul II. In 1969, as Cardinal Wojtyła, he published his major philosophical work, *The Acting Person*. In it, the future pope emphasized the *moral act* on the stage of life. Faith must express itself in action.

Both Reagan and John Paul II knew this. Despite their unshakable faith and their belief in the Divine Plan, they understood that humans retained free will and that therefore they needed the courage to act in the real world. The pope and the president both saw their mission as to try to do God's will according to a Divine Plan.

In his encyclical *Sollicitudo Rei Socialis* (1987), John Paul II insisted that human beings must seek to do God's will with the talents they have received. The pope wrote, "Anyone wishing to renounce the difficult yet noble task of improving the lot of man in his totality, and of all people, with the excuse that the struggle is difficult and that constant effort is required, or simply because of the experience of defeat and the need to begin again, that person would be betraying the will of God the Creator." He concluded, "It falls to us, who receive the gifts of God in order to make them fruitful, to 'sow' and 'reap.'"[13]

Ronald Reagan believed this, too. After surviving his assassination attempt, he said, "Whatever time I have left is for Him."

The pope and the president thus found themselves acting in a larger *theo-drama*, to borrow the apt description offered by one of the sources interviewed for this book, Bishop Robert Barron.

Both the pope and the president found meaning in their lives and in their ultimate platforms. On the global stage in the 1980s, they sought to defeat a terrible ideology. It would require performances of a lifetime.

That story—*their* story—is a gripping one. The stakes are high, with hundreds of millions of people suffering under murderous Marxist-Leninist regimes. It is a story with highs and lows, twists and turns, good guys and bad guys—life and death.

Let's watch it unfold.

ACT I

1

THE GRAND STAGE

June 2, 1979. The setting is Poland. An Iron Curtain has descended across Eastern Europe.

Right now, however, that curtain has let in a crack of light. That is because there, before more than a million Poles, stands their star. He is not a matinee idol, though he was an actor in his youth. He is the pope—the first Polish pope in history, a hero to this devout Catholic populace. Pope John Paul II, born and raised in Poland as Karol Wojtyła, sends chills down the spines of his countrymen as he exhorts them to be not afraid of the guns and tanks of atheistic Communism.

This is the Slavic pope's debut in his native land. He holds forth in Warsaw's Victory Square. The ex-actor has made a perfect choice of location, for this moment sets in motion forces that, a decade later, will secure victory in the Cold War. The Iron Curtain will fall.

Thousands of miles westward, a man with an audience of one senses the importance of the moment.

Ronald Reagan, another ex-actor, sits in his California home with Richard V. Allen, his future national security adviser in the White House. After a lengthy meeting, they decide to turn on the evening news. When footage of the pope in Victory Square comes on the TV, Reagan is transfixed.

The former governor remains silent as he watches the massive crowds celebrate the pope. He is astonished to see such a mass outpouring of emotion behind the Iron Curtain.

Allen glances over at Reagan and notices something unusual and unexpected: a tear in his eye.

"Dick, that's it," Reagan suddenly announces. "That's it. The pope is the key! We have got to find a way to reach out to this pope and the Vatican and make them an ally."

Of course, to do that, this other ex-actor needs to pull off an extraordinary performance of his own: he needs to get elected president of the United States.

That is not an easy role to land. In the not-too-distant future, however, he will claim it. And he will begin an extraordinary partnership with the headliner in Victory Square.

"EVERYTHING HAPPENS FOR A REASON"

Did Ronald Reagan and John Paul II's partnership emerge as part of a Divine Plan?

The two partners would have seen it that way.

These men, so different in so many ways, and raised continents apart, shared core convictions that stemmed from their respective religious faiths. Not least, they believed in Divine Providence.

This fact would have surprised most Reagan observers during his presidency. Even today, most historians disregard Reagan's faith and religious thought. But this actor-turned-president possessed a strong sense of God's role in almost everything that unfolds in the course of human events. "I've always believed that we were, each of us, put here for a reason, that there is a plan, somehow a divine plan for all of us," President Reagan told an audience at the National Prayer Breakfast in February 1982.[1]

He acquired that outlook as a young man from his devout mother, a faithful servant of the Disciples of Christ denomination. "Everything happens for a reason," Nelle Reagan told her son.[2]

This pious disciple of Christ taught her boy over and over that everything that happens in life, good or bad, does so according to a divine plan by a loving God.

Reagan recalled of his mother: "She had an abiding faith in the necessity to believe and trust that everything that happens, happens for some good reason, and while you can't always see the reason at the moment, it happens for the best. She believed that if a person does have this kind of faith in God and faces up to the situation without rebellion or bitterness and is willing to wait for a time, he will learn the reason and discover its place in the divine scheme of things."[3]

Nelle and her boy were echoing the Apostle Paul: "And we know that in all things God works for the good of those who love him, who have been called according to his purpose" (Romans 8:28).

How could observers have missed this about Reagan? Well, they did—probably owing to the secularism so common to biographers, historians, and journalists. Many of them missed it even as Reagan made it plain in his memoirs, published in 1990, only a year after he left the White House. In that book he repeatedly credited God with interventions along his path.

On occasion after occasion in telling his life story, Reagan would interject: "Then, one of those things happened that makes one wonder about God having a plan for all of us...." In Reagan's estimation, a caring Creator both opened and closed doors for him. God surely turned away the young Reagan from that dream job at Montgomery Ward, the older Reagan assured us in his memoirs. God just as surely placed that new teacher with a knack for teaching acting at Dixon High School just as Reagan arrived there. Coincidence? Not to Reagan. "Once again fate intervened," Reagan interpreted, "as if God was carrying out His plan with my name on it."[4]

This core belief proved central to the bond he shared with Karol Wojtyła, who learned such a theology in his parents' home.

Reagan would have agreed with John Paul II's well-known aphorism "In the designs of Providence there are no mere coincidences." The pontiff expressed this idea in Fátima, Portugal, on May 13, 1982, exactly one year after Mehmet Ali Agca attempted to assassinate him on the feast day of Our Lady of Fátima.[5] The pope had gone to Fátima to give thanks to the Blessed Mother for the protection of a heavenly hand. The heavens—the divine will—had spared him.

Fátima, the pope would say later, "helps us see the hand of God."

George Weigel, the leading biographer of John Paul II, emphasizes the importance of this statement. Weigel told us that the pope "was profoundly convinced of a truth" he articulated at Fátima. The biographer explains what the pope meant by his famous statement that there are no coincidences in God's plan: "What we perceive as coincidences or randomness is simply some facet of the Divine Plan that we haven't fit into the picture frame yet. But God is ultimately in charge of history. And God is quite capable, through his providential guidance of history, of cleaning up messes that human beings have made."

That, Weigel says, is the fundamental message of Jesus Christ in history: "God is making history turn back into its proper direction. But whether you are a Christian or not, John Paul II thought you could understand the notion that there is divine purpose at work in human affairs." Weigel adds that John Paul II believed that the "task of *conscience*, a word of great value in Western civilization, is to determine what that divine purpose is and then to live it out irrespective of the cost."

FREE WILL AND DIVINE DESTINY

Although Reagan and John Paul II believed in Divine Providence, they also believed that humans retain free will. They understood that the Creator has granted each person a conscience, and that this conscience is there to be used. Human beings must seek to cooperate with the divine purpose in the historical choices they make.

The historians, theologians, and scholars we interviewed for this book spoke at length about Reagan and John Paul II's understanding of free will and divine destiny, of the enigmatic interplay between the created and the Creator.

"Ronald Reagan had a large religious streak to him," notes Douglas Brinkley, who saw that streak in *The Reagan Diaries.* "He communicated with God, he felt like he was a tool of God, as he saw it, and this gave him a kind of strength. He never felt alone, he never was in despair. When we wonder why Reagan was avuncular all the time, it's because he felt that he had a proper relationship with God, knew his time was limited, and was going to proceed with a kind of divine guidance."

Reagan did indeed proceed that way. Journalists who paid close attention would have seen it. As far back as his gubernatorial years, in the late 1960s, *Newsweek* reported that Reagan saw himself as "His [God's] instrument."[6]

To many people in our rapidly secularizing culture, such a belief—that he saw himself as a *tool of God*—might come off as arrogant and self-important. But as devout religious believers understand, seeking to be an instrument of God is the opposite of prideful. A man humbles himself by submitting his will to God's will. To *go it alone* would be arrogant and self-important, since it would mean believing that he had all the right answers.

Reagan's humility was clear to his associates. Bill Clark, Reagan's closest aide and spiritual partner, often said of Reagan, "There was no pride there at all." Clark explained: "His number one maxim [was] that we can accomplish anything if we don't concern ourselves with who gets the credit.... He just had total confidence in the Divine Will. He was there as an instrument of God, and one of many.... This was an amazingly humble person. True humility."[7]

Reagan and Clark prayed the Peace Prayer of St. Francis together. That famous prayer begins, "Lord, make me an instrument of your peace." There are fewer more renowned examples of humility before and subservience to the Almighty than Francis of

Assisi, admired by believers and nonbelievers alike. Countless millions have prayed that prayer in their churches. Reagan did, too. He prayed it because he meant it.

When we interviewed John O'Sullivan, who wrote a book on Reagan, John Paul II, and British prime minister Margaret Thatcher, he began with this caveat: "I am not a theologian, I'm a journalist." But he continued: "It does seem to me that, yes, God does have a plan, but we are capable of frustrating His plan. We can, for example, decide to go to hell. That is not what He wants for us, but we can do it. And it is fairly clear, I think, that neither Stalin nor Hitler were following what God wanted from their lives. So, what does it mean to say God has a plan, if we can frustrate it? I think it means that He hopes, [that] He would like, certain events to happen. He wants us always to behave virtuously, decently, in a kind way and thinking of others before ourselves."

And yet, O'Sullivan says, humans are able, through ignorance or malice or folly, to diverge from this plan. "So, from a historical point of view, and from a historian's point of view, I think we don't sort of go around asking the question what is God's plan for Hitler, Stalin, Reagan, Thatcher, the pope. We analyze what actually happened on the ground and we draw what I would describe as commonsense conclusions about how God is working in history."

The role of the historian, the biographer, and surely the theologian is to look back and try to interpret what happened. But modern historians and biographers shy away, if not recoil, from the "commonsense conclusions" O'Sullivan mentioned—despite the fact that the two main protagonists in this drama interpreted events through a theological prism.

Pointing to the March 1981 assassination attempt on Reagan, O'Sullivan notes that the president emerged from it strengthened in his conviction "that he had been put on Earth for a great purpose." O'Sullivan continues: "It strengthened his decision to try to do the right thing. I don't think it gave him specific instructions, but it did [give him the sense that] 'The rest of my life belongs to the big fellow upstairs.'"

O'Sullivan does not speculate here. Reagan articulated this perspective often, privately and publicly. While he was in the hospital recuperating from the shooting, he told Bill Clark that he believed God had spared his life for a special purpose. Reagan said the same to his children Maureen and Michael. White House aides such as Kenneth Duberstein, Lyn Nofziger, and Michael Deaver spoke of the president's sense of having been saved for a specific purpose.[8]

When Reagan got out of the hospital, he recorded the sentiment in his diary. "I know it's going to be a long recovery," he wrote. "Whatever happens now I owe my life to God and will try to serve him in every way I can."[9]

Less than three weeks after the shooting, on Good Friday 1981, Reagan visited with a Catholic cardinal: Terence Cooke, the archbishop of New York. "The hand of God was upon you," Cooke told Reagan. Reagan agreed, saying simply, "I know." He then told Cooke: "I have decided that whatever time I have left is for Him."[10]

A successor to Cardinal Cooke, Cardinal Timothy Dolan, spoke to us for this book. The archbishop of New York is not only one of the leading prelates of the Roman Catholic Church but also a historian and a self-described "aficionado" of Ronald Reagan. Dolan also lived through and studied the life of Karol Wojtyła.

"Ronald Reagan and certainly John Paul II would have had a providential view of history," says Dolan. "In the famous words of John Paul II, who survived two brushes with death, a coincidence is what a believer calls *Divine Providence*. So, in the view of reality of both of these towering men, Ronald Reagan and John Paul II, there were no accidents." Dolan observes that both men shared a worldview that he characterizes this way: "Things were going to work out slowly, gradually, according to God's plan. History is *His* story, *God's* story."

Dolan notes that Reagan would have gotten this view from his mother: "He was very quick to [assert] that view of the world that everything is in God's hands. And obviously, John Paul II got [that view] from his deep Catholic faith and his love of God's revealed word in the Bible. That intense personal conviction that God was in charge—that conviction was only deepened by the fact that they were both spared death in serious assassination attempts."

"Whatever He Accomplished Was God's Will"

Reagan reflected the influence of his mother throughout his life. A radio colleague from the early 1930s—well before Reagan got to Hollywood—remembered, "He was a deeply religious man." This friend recalled Reagan as "not the kid who went to church every Sunday" but nonetheless as "a man with a strong inner faith. Whatever he accomplished was God's will—God gave it to him and God could take it away."[11]

We see this thinking throughout Reagan's long life, especially in letters he wrote. As governor of California and then president of the United States, he reached out to grieving widows and mothers, trying to comfort them with assurances that God has a plan for the best, even if we cannot always understand it in this lifetime. When a New York woman wrote Governor Reagan about the struggles of her handicapped son, he replied, "Things have a way of working out in life, and usually for the best, if we simply go forward doing our best and trusting that God does have a plan."[12]

Governor Reagan told another woman that we need to be content in "bearing what we cannot change and going on with what God has given us, confident there is a destiny."[13]

He also reached out to the widow of a slain police officer, telling her that no one can be sure of "the why of God's plan for us." He continued: "Whatever God's plan is for each of us, we can only trust in His wisdom and mercy.... It isn't given to us to understand—we can only have faith.... We must have faith in God's plan for all of us."[14]

Reagan applied this thinking when considering his own death. He once told his daughter Patti, who was not especially religious, that he used to fear dying in an airplane crash. He overcame those fears, he said, by taking comfort in his confidence in God's goodness. The conversation began when Patti asked her father why he prayed each time he boarded an airplane:

> "Do you pray that the plane won't crash?" I asked him, assuming that would be a logical thing for which to pray.
>
> "No," he answered. "I pray that whatever God's will is, I'll be able to accept it with grace, and have faith in His wisdom. We're always in God's hands. Sometimes it's hard to accept that, so I pray that He'll help me just to trust in His will."...
>
> What my father had communicated to me, through his words and between them, was that he believed God was in charge of his fate and the fate of everyone on the plane. He had told me once before that when we die is God's business. So it wasn't his place to second-guess God or try to sell Him a particular agenda by praying, "Please don't let the plane crash."
>
> And I thought of this, too: If I were falling through the sky, falling toward my death, would I want my last moments to be spent screaming at God for not obeying my wishes, or would I want to exit this earth in a moment of silent communion, a prayer for grace and acceptance? The latter definitely seemed like a better way to go.
>
> My father has chosen, on a daily basis, to try to accept the will of God.[15]

Reagan believed wholeheartedly not only in God's will but also that one could not know God's will ahead of time, and could only seek counsel through prayer. "Whatever the outcome, it will be His doing," Reagan said in 1976, and many times before and after. "I will pray for understanding of what it is He would have me do."[16]

Trying to solve the mystery of God's will is a challenge for humans in any era. It haunted the men of Reagan's and John Paul II's time. Whittaker Chambers, who struggled to pull himself up from the pit of atheistic Communism, wrote of the difficulty of the process in his groundbreaking 1952 memoir, *Witness*, a book Reagan could quote passages from verbatim. "I did not seek to know God's will," Chambers wrote. "I did not suppose that anyone could know God's will. I only sought prayerfully to know and to do God's purpose with me."[17]

That describes what Ronald Reagan and John Paul II sought, too.

After being brought up in the Disciples of Christ denomination, Reagan as an adult became a member of Bel Air Presbyterian Church in Hollywood. Many would argue that Reagan's sense of God's sovereignty had a Presbyterian-Calvinist element to it. But Scott Hahn, a former Reformed Calvinist and one of America's best-known converts to Catholicism, objects to the idea that Reagan's thinking accorded with a "very Calvinist sense" of thinking. He told us that he sees the president's perspective instead as "very Augustinian." It was a matter of the role of man and God within the dimensions of good and evil. It was a matter of free will within the framework of the sovereignty of God.[18]

Bill Clark agreed. The Reagan adviser, who spent time in an Augustinian novitiate considering the priesthood, saw the president's approach as a matter of discernment. That is the overriding challenge for the Christian: to decipher and reconcile one's own sense of lived experiences with God's will.

Clark, from his time in the novitiate, was familiar with the process of discernment in the spiritual exercises of St. Ignatius of Loyola. Another person interviewed for this book, Bishop Robert Barron, points to St. Ignatius's classic discernment language: *What does God want me to do?*

Barron, well known as host of the PBS documentary series *Catholicism* and as founder of Word on Fire Catholic Ministries, is at ease digging into "Divine Plan" theology. He points to the stories of King David in the Scriptures, noting how one sees God intervene throughout. David can choose or not choose to cooperate with God's will. In a statement that applies as much to Reagan, John Paul II, and the rest of us as it does to David, Barron says:

Well, what does God want me to do? I'm following the prompt of what I think is God's will, but I'm testing. I'm discerning as I go. The main thing is, am I following the path of love? Because God is love. Whatever God's purpose is, it is a loving purpose. Love means to will the good of the other. So every time I make a free decision, am I moving in the direction of willing the good of someone else? Then I know I'm basically on the right path. Then I also look for signs, indicators as I go. Is this what God wants me to do? And it's always that path of what enhances the life of someone around me.

Discernment is never an easy process. Even if one is a person of faith and has great confidence in God, one might know God's plan only in retrospect... if at all.

THE DIVINE PLAYWRIGHT THOUGHT IT WORTH THE RISK

As Bishop Barron puts it, the debate over God's role versus our role represents "one of the great issues in all of theology." It has occupied the best minds for thousands of years, from the days of Aristotle and Plato, through Augustine and Aquinas, up through modern thinkers.

Reagan frequently quoted C. S. Lewis, who mused about free will in his classic *Mere Christianity*.[19] Lewis averred that God gave people free will, meaning that He allows his creatures to go "either wrong or right." The creature is free to follow but also free to disobey. God did not want a world of machines or automated creatures. Lewis wrote, "Of course God knew what would happen if they used their freedom the wrong way: apparently He thought it worth the risk."

It was a risk that God was willing to accept in a dynamic creation. In *His* dynamic creation. For God "merely to over-ride a human will," Lewis stated, "would be for Him useless."[20]

Elsewhere Lewis wrote: "There are only two kinds of people in the end: those who say to God, 'Thy will be done,' and those to whom God says, in the end, '*Thy* will be done.' All that are in Hell, choose it. Without that self-choice there could be no Hell."[21]

Obviously, God can do all things, with or without a certain person, but he offers his grace and desires the person's assent, his cooperation, his *yes*, given through the person's free will. As Augustine put it, "God who created you without you, will not save you without you."

The most widely watched and read American Catholic of C. S. Lewis's day was Bishop Fulton Sheen, who was raised in a small town near where Reagan was raised, and who met John Paul II shortly after he assumed the papacy. In his classic *Peace of Soul*, Sheen asserted, "God refuses to be a totalitarian dictator in order to abolish evil by destroying human freedom."

Sheen regretted that too many people blame God for the bad things that happen but not the good. "The only time some men...ever think of God," Sheen said, "is when they want to find someone to blame for their own sins. Without ever saying so, they assume that man is responsible for everything good and beautiful in the world, but God is responsible for its wickedness and its wars."

Sheen added, "They ignore the fact that God is like a playwright who wrote a beautiful drama, gave it to men to act with all the directions for acting, and they made a botch of it."[22]

The noted Catholic philosopher Peter Kreeft, who converted from Dutch Reformed Calvinism, has similarly addressed free will and predestination:

> Every good story has a sense of destiny, of fittingness as if it were written by God. But every story also leaves its characters free. Lesser writers may jimmy and force their characters into molds, but the greater the writer the more clearly the reader sees that his characters are real people and not just mental concepts. The more nearly the characters have a life of their

own and seem to leap off the page into real life, the greater a writer we have. God, of course, is the greatest writer of all.[23]

Because human life is His story—God's story—it must have *both* destiny and freedom. God, being omniscient, already knows how the story ends. He knows how each of our stories ends. But our free will, Kreeft writes, "follows from the divine love," for "to love someone is to make them free."

Few theologians believe in *pure* free will; most believe in and assume God's grace. But to deny human free will would be to deny something essential to the Christian life: personal responsibility. Sounding like a mix of C. S. Lewis and Fulton Sheen, Kreeft asserts: "If I am a robot, even a divinely programmed robot, my life no longer has the drama of real choice and turns into a formula, the unrolling of a prewritten script. God loves me too much to allow that. He would sooner compromise His power than my freedom." Kreeft adds: "Actually, He does neither. It is precisely His power that gives me my freedom."[24]

Bishop Barron agrees. "The Catholic tradition," he remarks, "has always said that [God's Providence and human freedom] are really mutually implicative." God "has a plan, but He wants us cooperating with it." According to Barron: "The main point is that it's not a zero-sum game [by which] the more God does, the less we do, or the more we're involved with, the less God is involved. No, on the contrary."

According to Cardinal Dolan, John Paul II and Reagan shared this perspective. Dolan says that the pope would often quote a famous statement by the second-century theologian St. Irenaeus: "The glory of God is man fully alive." John Paul II understood that "we are hard-wired for the divine," Dolan observes, and we must live our lives in consonance with the Divine Author's plans and guidance. "I know Reagan would not have used those words," the cardinal adds, "but Reagan would certainly believe in the dignity of the human person and that government existed to protect the freedom that the human person needed."

Barron likewise cites Irenaeus's statement but also notes that Christianity says "that the goal of the human life is to become divinized, to be drawn into God's own nature, own life." The bishop continues: "I don't care if you are proposing something in the economic order, the political order, the cultural order, no one has got a better humanism, a more complete humanism than Christianity. Both John Paul II and Ronald Reagan, as deeply believing Christians, I think got that."

In short, free will and destiny are two sides of the same coin. Such a viewpoint is not strictly a Catholic one, as the cases of Ronald Reagan (a Presbyterian) and C. S. Lewis (an Anglican) suggest. Peter Kreeft makes this point when he writes, "I think we can do as much justice to the sovereignty of God as a Calvinist and as much justice to the free will of man as a Baptist."[25]

THEO-DRAMA

All the world's a stage for all of us. We all have our own dramas. But life, for the person who believes in a loving God that helps direct us according to His purposes, is a grander *theo-drama*.

That's a term Bishop Barron uses frequently and finds well suited to describing the lives of Ronald Reagan and Pope John Paul II. Once a person asks the fundamental question *What does God want me to do?*, that person sees his role as living in service of others.

Barron says: "I think John Paul and Ronald Reagan both had that sense as they did battle with Communism. They saw what they were doing was enhancing the lives of all kinds of people. That's the great indicator that you are involved in the theo-drama the way God wants you to be."

That was certainly how John Paul II and Reagan saw their roles, especially after both nearly died at the hands of would-be assassins in the spring of 1981. Each man believed that God had intervened to spare his life. Reagan said explicitly and emphatically that his life purpose thereafter would be directed to the honor and glory and guidance of God.

Both Reagan and John Paul II wanted to believe that they were God's instruments. They believed, too, that the Divine Plan applied to nations, not just to individuals. The pope professed his "conviction that the destiny of all nations lies in the hands of a merciful Providence."[26] So did Reagan, especially regarding America's role in the world. Reagan quoted a remark from Pope Pius XII many times throughout his life: "Into the hands of America, God has placed an afflicted mankind."[27]

Reagan spoke that way many years before he entered politics. In a June 1952 commencement address, the Hollywood actor said, "I believe that God in shedding his grace on this country has always in this divine scheme of things kept an eye on our land and guided it as a promised land."[28] As president three decades later, he reaffirmed, "I've always believed that this blessed land was set apart in a special way, that some divine plan placed this great continent here between the two oceans to be found by people from every corner of the Earth—people who had a special love for freedom."[29]

To be sure, Reagan and John Paul II—the head of state and the head of the largest Christian denomination—had different emphases and motivations. "In Pope John Paul II's point of view," Cardinal Dolan says, "his major goal in life was not to bring down the Iron Curtain. His major mission in life was to proclaim Jesus Christ as the way of truth and the life, the son of God and our savior. If that was proclaimed effectively, the other would happen." As for Reagan, Dolan says, it was a grandiose mission, embodied by his "Shining City on a Hill" rhetoric and Manifest Destiny vision of America, "to protect freedom . . . to protect it from Communist tyranny."

But their shared core convictions allowed them to unite on an issue of world-historical importance. "Reagan and Pope John Paul II rise on the same tide," says Douglas Brinkley, "and the tide's not just anti-Communism." In the end, Brinkley says, each man stood not merely "against something" but also in "favor of something." Brinkley underscores their "shared optimism." That optimism "embraced the idea that millions of people trapped behind a wall of oppression would welcome a message of human dignity and freedom, and emerge at the end with the ability to rule themselves."

Few at the time felt that such a scenario could realistically come to pass. But John Paul II and Ronald Reagan stayed true to their vision.

2

THE ACTING PERSONS

B oth Karol Wojtyła and Ronald Reagan had been actors and had dabbled in poetry since their youth. Wojtyła, in his time, was known to be a more promising poet and playwright, while Reagan held the renown as an actor. Both performed in theater, with Reagan going on to movies and television in Hollywood's Golden Age. Both enjoyed the craft and gave it up only reluctantly.

The similarities extend beyond the superficial. Notably, both discovered that their acting skills helped them in their roles on the world stage.

THE IMPORTANCE OF ACTING

Reagan, when asked how an actor could become president, quipped that he wondered how anyone could be president *without* having been an actor.

This line always prompted a laugh, but it also represented a shrewd observation. Reagan knew that his acting experience served him well.

"The common criticism of Reagan was that he was just an actor," notes Reagan biographer H. W. Brands. "What did he know about politics? Well, Reagan understood very well that having been an actor served him exceedingly usefully in politics."

The same was true for Karol Wojtyła once he became pope. He probably did not expect his training in the theater to help with papal functions, but that turned out to be the case. A high school friend, Halina Kwiatkowska, said she believed that "his theatrical experience gave him his strong voice and magnificent direction, shaped his beautiful sense of gesture, taught him to appreciate the value of a pause, suitable for homilies." She added that the theater developed in the future pope an "ease" of connecting with an audience "and especially an ability to express the inner truth in a convincing manner."[1]

Cold War historian Stephen Kotkin agrees. "Both Reagan and Pope John Paul II were able to win over mass audiences, which looks a lot easier to say than it is to do," Kotkin says. "They had a kind of personal touch, but that personal touch could extend to very large numbers of people. In the case of the pope, he wasn't really a television personality, per se, although he had the acting background. Reagan, of course, had the television personality experience. But both of them very effectively commanded the public sphere." Echoing Kwiatkowska, Kotkin notes that they knew how to "make telling gestures, [employ] pauses in their speech, using a very effective language and metaphor, knowing their audiences well, and capturing those audiences."

James Rosebush, a senior adviser to President Reagan, says: "Having been actors put them in a position of understanding the audience, and the first thing about being an effective speaker or communicator is an appreciation for and love of your audience, whether you're seeing the audience through the lens of a camera or whether you're speaking to a live audience of millions of people. You have to build a bridge to your audience. Ronald Reagan and Pope John Paul II were masters at this."

Similarly, Bishop Robert Barron sees theatrical experience as a key factor in what made Reagan and John Paul II such successful leaders:

I think the fact that both Ronald Reagan and John Paul II were actors matters a lot for a lot of different reasons. But one of them was they both knew how to inhabit the stage. And they both knew how to use some of the technology available to them. Reagan was famously the Great Communicator. I remember as a young man watching Ronald Reagan on television, watching him give a speech, and yes indeed, he was a great communicator. John Paul II, when you heard him speaking other languages—Polish, French, Italian, or English— you wouldn't have that same polished sort of Reaganesque thing, but nevertheless, John Paul II had an intensity about him and he knew how to, I think, use his voice and use his eyes and use his posture in a way that was very riveting.

Barron retains a vivid memory of watching John Paul II come to Washington and seeing him standing in the car, moving through the crowd, in red cape and white cassock: "It was just the way he bore himself. It was a bit like Anthony Hopkins or one of the great stage actors who know how to stand. I've noticed that with the great actors it is not just speaking but they know how to stand on a stage, where most of us would feel fidgety and uncomfortable. John Paul had that quality. He knew how to inhabit a public space."

Barron points out that St. Peter's Basilica in Rome, and particularly the spot where the pope holds forth from the Chair of St. Peter, is effectively "a stage set." Watch any Christmas Mass or special solemnity Mass at the Vatican and you will notice what a finely orchestrated production it is, with the pope's every step mapped out. John Paul II "knew how to inhabit that space very effectively," Barron says.

Something else distinguished these two actors performing on the global stage: they believed what they conveyed, and they felt they had an important message to deliver. Kotkin speaks of their "moral stance—that is to say, the principles and values by which they stood." And like the Apostle Paul, they knew that to communicate deeply held beliefs requires not only telling but also *showing.* Paul says *follow (imitate) me as I follow Christ.* Using the right words is not enough. You must model the behavior; you must play the role so observers can learn a deeper truth. The ancient Greeks recognized this, too: Plato and Aristotle spoke of *mimesis*—of imitating the true, the good, and the beautiful.[2]

In a remarkable *Letter to Artists*, Pope John Paul II affirmed: "Not all are called to be artists in the specific sense of the term. Yet, as Genesis has it, all men and women are entrusted with the task of crafting their own life: in a certain sense, they are to make of it a work of art, a masterpiece."[3]

Analyzing this letter, philosophy professor Daniel McInerny writes: "He began wanting to be an actor, but he ended up playing a role in a rather different drama. We human beings are, in a real sense, all actors in a drama in which we either achieve, or fail to achieve, our happiness. It is a drama in which God, as the young Karol Wojtyła learned, is the chief protagonist. Our task is to play the role that He assigns to us. And to do our best, no matter what challenges and disruptions come, never to break character."[4]

The key lesson here is that the *actions* of the actor carry meaning. Karol Wojtyła and Ronald Reagan understood this. In taking a stand against Communism, they repeatedly conveyed an internal truth with an outward action. As we will see, such actions marked some of the most dramatic moments in their public roles.

George Weigel underscores how acting taught the pope and the president more than just practical skills such as how to deliver a line well or how to connect with an audience. Weigel explains:

> I think they both took from that theatrical experience perhaps a view of life as well. I know this is true of John Paul II. He thought of life as a drama. Life is lived in the gap between the person I am today and the person I really ought to be. That is an inherently dramatic situation, trying to close that gap with the help of God's grace is an inherently dramatic business. So life itself is a kind of drama. And that gave him a richly textured sense of the human condition. It gave him a

great human compassion because everybody is living in that gap between the person I am and the person I ought to be. And while Reagan, I don't think, would have put it in those semi-philosophical or theological terms, I think he had the same sense too. Being on stage for him was not simply a matter of performing. His performance as president was trying to close that gap between what America was and what America ought to be, between what the world was and what the world ought to be.

Weigel adds that John Paul II brought to the papacy "an idea of drama, of the theater, as a kind of privileged place for revealing and understanding the human condition in all of its complexity." Why do people still perform Shakespeare centuries after his death? "Because the things that people do or don't do in Shakespeare's plays revealed deep truths about who we are as human beings, how we should live, how we shouldn't live."

James Rosebush saw up close why Reagan flourished in his public role. "If you encounter most actors off camera," Rosebush says, "they can be the opposite of the character they're actually engaged to portray. Sometimes they're inarticulate. They may understand more about the character they're playing than they understand about themselves." Reagan was just the opposite: he understood himself as well as his audience. "He was the same off camera as he was on camera," Rosebush says. "That is why he was accorded this title 'The Great Communicator,' because what you saw on camera was exactly what his character was. And for me, having an opportunity to see him in all different kinds of situations that were not formal, where he was not on camera, traveling the world with him, sitting in the back seat of limousines and motorcade rides, briefing him in his bedroom in his pajamas, [I saw] that the person of Ronald Reagan was the same as the one in front of the lens of a camera. He embraced the same ideas." Rosebush adds: "This gave Reagan an authenticity.... Reagan was a film actor, that's true, but he was much more than that. He was a person who came to film with character. He didn't have to assume the character of another person."

Shakespeare understood that playacting was almost a sacred human endeavor to know thyself. Here were two actors who knew themselves.

THE ACTOR-TURNED-POPE

John Paul II wrote his *Letter to Artists* in 1999. Thirty years earlier, as Cardinal Wojtyła, he published *The Acting Person*. This book is a major philosophical work in which Wojtyła looks at how each person acts out his or her life. The themes of *The Acting Person* carried into and throughout his papacy.

In the book, Wojtyła sets forth a theory of the person as a self-determining actor, or agent, who realizes his or her full human potential through action that is free but also responsible. This is not a libertarian view of freedom that exalts freedom itself as the highest good. Rather, Wojtyła outlines a Christian conception of freedom that insists the only truly authentic expression of freedom is a freedom coupled with faith. Christian guidelines, a Judeo-Christian framework, and a moral compass are essential to a proper expression of freedom. The human agent must seek to act out freedom within this structure. Only then can the human person, made in God's image, fully live out what he or she is made to be.

The Catholic faith, and particularly the Thomistic tradition, does not see the body as innately bad or depraved. God made us in His image, the *imago Dei*, and his only begotten son took on human flesh. Thomas Aquinas wrote: "We ought to cherish the body. Our body's substance is not from an evil principle, as the Manicheans imagine, but from God. And therefore we ought to cherish the body by the friendship of love, by which we love God." Because a particular human being is composed "of this soul, of this flesh, and of these bones," said Aquinas, "so it belongs to the notion of humanity to be composed of soul, flesh and bones."[5]

In his book on Aquinas, Bishop Barron connects this "rapport between flesh and spirit" to the human drama, just as Karol Wojtyła did. Barron writes: "And the human drama, this mystical journey into the divine, does not take place in some rarefied spiritual realm, cut off from earth, from color and relationship and sight and sound. Rather, it is an adventure of the entire person, of the embodied soul and the ensouled body, of the incarnate spirit that, in its strange beauty, uniquely mirrors something of God's being."[6]

Wojtyła emphasized the human person and the person's connection to the divine realm through the Father, Son, and Holy Spirit within this transition of life. He took an elevated view of the human body and the human person, both worth honoring and protecting.

Though not a Catholic, Ronald Reagan shared this higher vision of the person.

Wojtyła's understanding of the human person and the divine realm within this transition of life reflected his focus on "personalism."

The personalist movement arose out of the ashes of World War I, as various thinkers argued that depersonalized political, economic, and social systems had encroached on the dignity of the human person. Wojtyła picked up the concept and underscored the unity of the person across all dimensions of human experience. Through various chosen acts, the person both forms himself and transcends the here and now.

"Possessed with reason and free will," writes political scientist Thomas Rourke, "the person seeks vertical transcendence when he seeks to know the truth and act in accord with it." To interfere with this search for the truth, or to prevent a person from acting according to the demands of conscience—which oppressive governments do—is to deny people their right to responsible personhood. In his stirring encyclical *Centesimus Annus*, Rourke notes, John Paul II extended this personalism to all of society, insisting that modern society respect the person.[7]

Wojtyła's conception of the human person speaks not only to the dignity of the person but also to the person *living* as a person and within community. In an analysis of *The Acting Person*, the late Cardinal Avery Dulles observed: "Activity is not something strictly other than the person; it is the person coming to expression and constituting itself. Persons, moreover, are essentially social and oriented to life in community. They achieve themselves as persons by interaction, giving to others and receiving from them in turn." Wojtyła proposed a "theory of participation" that sought to reconcile the good of the community with that of its individual members. In Dulles's words: "All must contribute to the common good, which then redounds to the benefit of the individual members."[8]

This teaching on the common good contained within it an implicit critique of both radical individualism and, at the other end of the spectrum, Marxist collectivism. George Weigel explains: "Radical individualism is inadequate, because we only grow into our humanity through interaction with others. Collectivism strips the person of freedom, and thus of his or her personhood."[9] The very idea of what John Paul II repeatedly referred to as the "sanctity and dignity of the human person" was antithetical to Marxism. Ronald Reagan, for his part, frequently decried the Communists' use of the phrase "the masses" because it ignored if not obliterated the notion of the individuality of the person. Reagan observed that problem from afar, as a free person living in America; Wojtyła felt it up close, as an unfree person living in Poland.

In 1968, a year before *The Acting Person* was published, Wojtyła wrote to the renowned Catholic philosopher Henri de Lubac:

> I devote my very rare free moments to a work that is close to my heart and devoted to the metaphysical significance and the mystery of the PERSON [emphasis original]. It seems to me that the debate today is being played on that level. The evil of our times consists in the first place in a kind of degradation, indeed in a pulverization, of the fundamental uniqueness of each human person. This evil is even much more of

the metaphysical than of the moral order. To this disintegration, planned at times by atheistic ideologies, we must oppose, rather than sterile polemics, a kind of "recapitulation" of the mystery of the person.[10]

As Dulles explained, Cardinal Wojtyła identified the "doctrine of the person" as the Achilles' heel of the Polish Communist regime. As pope, he repeatedly said that the remarkable brutality of the twentieth century stemmed from a refusal to recognize the inherent value of the human person made in the image and likeness of God.[11] Like Ronald Reagan, he insisted that human powers should never infringe on God-given, inalienable rights.

So two men—one Catholic, one Protestant; one raised in Wadowice, Poland, the other in Dixon, Illinois—entered the world stage with shared ideas about how persons should act out, and be permitted by the state to act out, in human society. Both John Paul II and Ronald Reagan thought deeply about the freedom of and violations against the human person, about the nature of man and the state.

MORAL ACTION

Weigel set out to define in the simplest terms possible the notions Wojtyła expressed in *The Acting Person*. In his seminal 1999 biography of John Paul II, *Witness to Hope*, Weigel dubs *The Acting Person* Wojtyła's "major philosophical project." He notes that in the original Polish, Wojtyła's opus bears the title *Osoba i Czyn*, which translates to *Person and Act*. He calls *The Acting Person* "a bad translation." The difference between the two titles is notable. *Person and Act*, Weigel states, retains the tension between "subjective consciousness" and "objective reality" in which Wojtyła attempted to construct his thesis. By contrast, the title *The Acting Person* emphasizes only the subjective side of Wojtyła's analysis.[12]

The determination to see the whole of experience, to "get to the reality of things-as-they-are" (in Weigel's words), drew Wojtyła to a philosophical method known as "phenomenology." As a doctoral student he wrote a thesis on one of the most important thinkers on phenomenology, the German philosopher Max Scheler (1874–1928).

Getting at the essence of phenomenology is no simple task.[13] But as Weigel notes, "Despite the movement's complexities of analysis and terminology, understanding the basic program of the phenomenological movement is not difficult."[14] Citing the great modern Catholic mind Michael Novak, Weigel defines phenomenology as an effort to "bring back into philosophy everyday things, concrete wholes, the basic experiences of life as they come to us."

Phenomenology rests on an understanding that truth is a process learned through human experience.

Philosophers like Scheler and the movement's founder, Edmund Husserl (1859–1938), saw a problem: they believed philosophy had become disconnected from the nitty-gritty of everyday life. There was too much thinking about thinking, too little knowing anything about anything.

As Weigel points out, understanding phenomenology "is essential if one wants to get inside the mind and the thinking of Karol Wojtyła."[15] John Paul II himself said, "They try to understand me from outside. But I can only be understood from inside."[16]

Wojtyła's lasting contribution was to apply the framework of phenomenology to the *moral* act, or the reaction. The way in which we respond to things in our experience tells us something. "The moral act is a *real* act with real consequences," Weigel writes, "and to Wojtyła's mind Scheler had failed to come to grips with how moral choices actually shape a person."[17]

So when Wojtyła wrote *The Acting Person*—or *Person and Act*—he sought to synthesize the older Aristotelian-Thomistic "philosophy of being" with the "philosophy of consciousness" that he had analyzed in his dissertation on Scheler.[18]

For the record, Wojtyła was more Thomist than phenomenologist. Rocco Buttiglione, professor of political science at Rome's

Saint Pius V University and a member of the Pontifical Academy of Social Sciences, who has studied the early philosophical thought of Karol Wojtyła probably closer than anyone, says that Wojtyła merely drew or borrowed from Scheler, while always philosophizing with "the light of St. Thomas Aquinas."[19] Or, as another scholar, Douglas Flippen of Christendom College, puts it, Wojtyła saw a "usefulness" in Scheler and in phenomenology's focus on intuition and experience, and yet it remains clear "that the philosophical view of reality of Pope John Paul II was firmly rooted in the metaphysics of St. Thomas Aquinas."[20]

Like the early thinkers of phenomenology, Wojtyła concerned himself with how to study human ethics without falling into the trap of solipsism—again, merely thinking about thinking. In Weigel's words, "How could modernity avoid a cul-de-sac of radical skepticism about the human capacity to know *anything* with certitude?"[21]

In *Person and Act*, Weigel says, Wojtyła examines how our thinking about the world and about ourselves "helps to understand ourselves as *persons*." Although some things in life simply "happen" to us, in other, more critical experiences we seem to know that we are deliberately making an important decision and acting out that decision. Weigel explains that in those particular experiences we come to truly know ourselves—not simply as the product of some "jumble of emotions and sensory perceptions, but as a *person*, a subject.... Some things don't simply 'happen' to me. I am the *subject*, not merely the object, of actions. I make things happen, because I think through a decision and then freely act on it. Therefore, I am *somebody*, not simply something."[22]

Wojtyła then shows how, in moral action, that *somebody* is able to experience his or her own larger transcendence.

Professor Richard A. Spinello puts it this way: "According to John Paul II, we must always consider the person's moral actions from the perspective of the acting person. The goodness or badness of the acting person's behavior depends on what that person wills and chooses." To be is to act, and man thus determines via his actions the meaning and value of his being.[23]

Weigel elaborates on this idea:

I think what Wojtyła believed as a philosopher was that what we do counts. It's not insignificant that I choose A over B. Because that very choice shapes my character. It affects my possibilities down the line. Our soul, if you will, is created by the choices we make, by the acts that we do. Now, the theater embodies the truth of all of that on the stage. I mean, think of Shakespeare. People make good choices and bad choices and things happen because of that. So there is a parallelism between the sense that the truth of a person reveals itself in the acts that they accomplish or don't accomplish, and the moral life. So that's the connection, if you will, between John Paul II, former theater person, and John Paul II, philosopher, theologian, pope.

Following the thinking of Aristotle, Wojtyła proffers that a habituated series of actions determines a person's character. "If I keep doing this over and over and over again, I become a certain type of person," Bishop Barron explains. "So John Paul knew that each time I choose in freedom, I choose this, I'm becoming that person.... If I'm choosing in the bad way consistently, I'm creating a bad character." Barron then links these ideas to the pope's theatrical background:

Think about a character in a play: if you pick up a playbill, *Hamlet, Prince of Denmark*, well it's not going to tell you much about Hamlet. But you watch the play, you watch Hamlet move and speak and react. Now you're understanding his character. Well, in a similar way, we're going to adapt Shakespeare again.... All the world's a stage and we're all players on it. You're not going to learn a lot about me by reading the playbill. The playbill would only tell you that I'm Bishop Robert Barron, auxiliary bishop of Los Angeles. But over time watch me act. Watch what I do. Watch how I choose. Watch

how my freedom unfolds, and you'll see the kind of character
I am. John Paul got that in his bones.

Barron explains how this perspective on moral action con-
tributed to John Paul II's revulsion toward Communism: "What
was bugging him so much about Marxism was it was compelling
people to make all kinds of bad choices. It was pushing them down
roads they ought not go down. And it was thereby creating bad
characters. He wanted to create a world in which it was easier to
be good, where the conditions for the possibility of good character development were in place. That was one of the fundamental
struggles."

THE ROLE OF FREEDOM

Freedom is necessary to this process. Through our human freedom,
which God grants via the gift of free will, we choose to act, and
we can act morally or not morally. As Weigel notes by example, we
can choose to pay a debt or cheat on a debt. It is ultimately here,
in the exercise of the free choice between what is good and what
is not, that we can discern the transcendence of the human person. As Weigel states: "I go beyond myself. I grow as a *person*, by
realizing my freedom and conforming it to the good and the true.
Through my freedom, I narrow the gap between the person-I-am
and the person-I-ought-to-be."[24]

In his interview for this book, Weigel told us that the all-
too-popular American and Western notion of freedom as "just
doing my own thing" reflects a "two-year-old's understanding of
freedom." Freedom is not mere license. Wojtyła had a "nobler idea"
of freedom, Weigel says: "Freedom is not just what I want to do.
Freedom is a matter of doing the right thing and doing that as a
matter of habit. That's a genuinely human freedom." A proper and
"mature" understanding links freedom to truth and goodness and
thus gives freedom a "certain nobility." This "was deeply engrained

in John Paul II from his experience," Weigel adds. "He knew that as a philosopher, as a theologian, as a man of the Bible, as a man of the church. But first of all, he knew it from experience. He knew it from his Polish experience during the Second World War and under the Communist regime."

Wojtyła expanded on his understanding of freedom as pope. In his first encyclical, *Redemptor Hominis* (1979), John Paul II called for people to seek "authentic freedom" and to "avoid every kind of illusory freedom, every superficial unilateral freedom, every freedom that fails to enter into the whole truth about man and the world."[25]

One of the pope's most important encyclicals was his August 1993 statement, *Veritatis Splendor*. There he wrote, "The relationship between man's freedom and God's law is most deeply lived out in the 'heart' of the person, in his moral conscience." He challenged the "cultural tendencies" by which "freedom and law are set in opposition to each other and kept apart, and freedom is exalted almost to the point of idolatry."[26]

John Paul II often described that "idolatry" of freedom, a near-worship of freedom for its own sake. Freedom should not be treated as the highest end, or virtue; the highest end, or virtue, is how one *acts* with the gift of that freedom. Freedom comes with a moral responsibility insisted on by the very Author of Life and Liberty. Moreover, no system or regime should deprive people of the freedom bequeathed by a loving God.

"One finds in John Paul II a protest against mistaken notions of freedom," writes Spinello. "Freedom that is not oriented to the good is not authentic freedom, but license and anarchy."[27]

Similarly, Bishop Barron says: "Our freedom is not absolute, but it's always seen in relationship to the truth. It finds itself in relation to the truth, and that's why the great political systems, such as ours, based upon freedom, relate to John Paul II absolutely. He sings the glories of freedom, but always freedom in relation to the truth, which means finally in relation to God. It's an ordered liberty, an ordered freedom."

John Paul II said precisely that while standing beside Ronald Reagan in Miami in September 1987. "From the beginning of America, freedom was directed to forming a well-ordered society and to promoting its peaceful life," the pope said. "Freedom was channeled to the fullness of human life, to the preservation of human dignity and to the safeguarding of human rights." He declared, in an exhortation that Reagan must have loved, that "this is the freedom that America is called to live and guard and to transmit." It was, he said, "ordered freedom."

"The only true freedom, the only freedom that can truly satisfy, is the freedom to do what we ought as human beings created by God according to his plan," John Paul II continued. "It is the freedom to live the truth of what we are and who we are before God, the truth of our identity as children of God, as brothers and sisters in common humanity. That is why Jesus Christ linked truth and freedom together."[28]

Reagan reciprocated. Whereas John Paul referred to the American Founding Fathers (virtually all of them Protestants), Reagan (a Protestant) quoted the Catholic philosopher Jacques Maritain on the Founders: "The Founding Fathers were neither metaphysicians nor theologians, but their philosophy of life and their political philosophy, their notion of natural law and of human rights, were permeated with concepts worked out by Christian reason." Reagan continued, "From the first, then, our nation embraced the belief that the individual is sacred and that as God himself respects human liberty, so, too, must the state."

The Founders believed that freedom of religion and of conscience were both sacred—more sacred than a man's castle, as James Madison put it. "The Religion then of every man must be left to the conviction and conscience of every man: and it is the right of every man to exercise it as these may dictate," wrote Madison, who called conscience "the most sacred of all property."

Cardinal Timothy Dolan remarks on this shared thinking of Reagan and John Paul II. He says that, to Reagan, "freedom was what was most important to the human person." And the president "would have found in Karol Wojtyła, in John Paul II, one nodding in agreement, philosopher of the human person that he was and faithful Catholic and believer that he was." A truly wise leader, Dolan notes, recognizes "that God has implanted in the human person a law of right and wrong."

And like John Paul II, Reagan believed that human beings had to properly exercise that precious gift of freedom with God's guidance. In a 1988 speech honoring Georgetown University's two hundredth anniversary, the president said, "At its full flowering, freedom is the first principle of society; this society, Western society." And yet, Reagan stressed, "freedom cannot exist alone. And that's why the theme for your bicentennial is so very apt: learning, faith, and freedom. Each reinforces the others, each makes the others possible. For what are they without each other?" The Protestant president asked his Catholic audience to pray that America be guided by learning, faith, and freedom. He continued: "[Alexis de] Tocqueville said it in 1835, and it's as true today as it was then: 'Despotism may govern without faith, but liberty cannot. Religion is more needed in democratic societies than in any other.'"[29]

Bishop Barron says: "I think both Ronald Reagan and John Paul II, from their Christian convictions, had this deep sense of freedom and dignity. And they realized the biblical roots of it: take the biblical roots away, those flowers are going to fade pretty quickly. And if you want evidence, look all around."

Societies need both faith and freedom. On that point as on so many other fundamentals, Reagan and John Paul II agreed.

In his first Christmas address as president, Reagan spoke of the "twin beacons of faith and freedom" that "have brightened the American sky." If the light of faith diminished in a state or society, then citizens would have to struggle to retain their freedom.

President Reagan made clear that the threats to both faith and freedom were real and growing. He told his national television audience that "the fate of a proud and ancient nation hangs in the balance." The people there, a people of "deep religious faith," had been "betrayed by their own government." An atheistic, totalitarian regime had declared martial law, answering "the stirrings of liberty with brute force, killings, mass arrests, and the setting up of concentration camps."

The nation Reagan referred to was John Paul II's native Poland. Those "stirrings of liberty" had begun when the pope made his triumphant return there two and a half years earlier—the appearance in Warsaw's Victory Square that brought a tear to Ronald Reagan's eye.

Just as Reagan watched the pope intently then, surely John Paul II was listening carefully to the American president now. By this point, less than a year into Reagan's presidency, the two leaders had already exchanged a dozen letters.[30] And through their public proclamations, they showed that they were closely aligned on bedrock principles—about faith and freedom, and human dignity, about the evil of atheistic Communism, and more.

Reagan had told his adviser Dick Allen in June 1979 that he needed to reach out to John Paul II and the Vatican and "make them an ally."

Now the alliance was forming. The partnership was growing. The Divine Plan was in motion.

PROCLAIMING AN EVIL EMPIRE

The extent to which Ronald Reagan and John Paul II aligned philosophically will surprise some readers. After all, John Paul II was not only a priest and a church leader but also an accomplished scholar who held two doctorates and taught at prestigious institutions. Reagan, by contrast, was never a scholar, and his critics have dismissed him as an intellectual lightweight. Wags said he "owned more horses than books."

But that caricature of Reagan has no basis in fact, as careful observers recognized at the time. Lee Edwards, the eminent historian of American conservatism, interviewed Reagan in 1965, even before the actor had become governor of California. Left alone in Reagan's library for a moment, Edwards began examining the books filling several large bookcases in the room. Edwards remembers: "They were, almost without exception, works of history, economics, and politics, including such conservative classics as F. A. Hayek's *The Road to Serfdom*, Whittaker Chambers's *Witness*, and Henry Hazlitt's *Economics in One Lesson*.... I opened several books—they were dog-eared and underlined. Here was the personal library not of a shallow Hollywood actor dangling at the end of someone's strings but of a thinking, reasoning individual who had arrived at his conservatism the old-fashioned way, one book at a time."[31]

Many close Reagan aides have attested to how closely Reagan studied issues—Bill Clark, Edwin Meese, Michael Deaver, and on and on.

Interviewed for this book, Reagan national security adviser Richard V. Allen says that the president "would study anything and everything." He tells a story to illustrate the point.

One day Allen handed Reagan the Communist publication *World Marxist Review*. The booklet ran to about a hundred pages, so the national security adviser used yellow tabs to mark a select few. He included a cover memorandum asking Reagan to read only the tabbed pages as part of his weekend reading at Camp David.

On Monday morning, Reagan told Allen, "What you gave me to read was absolutely riveting."

Allen replied, "So you read the tabbed pages, Mr. President?"

"No, I read the whole thing, cover to cover," Reagan said.

"That was his habit," Allen says.

Reagan even displayed some understanding of phenomenology, that complex field of philosophical study to which Karol Wojtyła devoted so much of his attention.

As president, Reagan actually used the word in one of his most famous speeches, and did so in a way that the Polish pontiff would have applauded.

Reagan mentioned phenomenology in his March 8, 1983, address to the National Association of Evangelicals, a group that was probably unfamiliar with the term. This speech is better known as Reagan's "Evil Empire" address.[32]

"We know that living in this world means dealing with what philosophers would call the phenomenology of evil or, as theologians would put it, the doctrine of sin," Reagan stated. "There is sin and evil in the world, and we're enjoined by Scripture and the Lord Jesus to oppose it with all our might."[33]

Reagan began by focusing on the sins of America—slavery, racism, ethnic hatred, religious bigotry—but toward the end of the speech he honed in on the locus of evil in the modern world.

"And this brings me to my final point today," Reagan said. He recalled his first presidential press conference, in which he had referred to Soviet leaders as dishonest men who "reserve unto themselves the right to commit any crime, to lie, to cheat."[34]

Note here the phenomenological focus on human action, on choice, and on the moral choice to do wrong.

Referring to Kremlin leaders, Reagan said, "While they preach the supremacy of the state, declare its omnipotence over individual man, and predict its eventual domination of all peoples on the Earth, they are the focus of evil in the modern world."

Pope John Paul II, victim of Communist state supremacy, of omnipotence over the individual, of domination of peoples, of evil, would have agreed with every word.

And John Paul II would have agreed with Reagan's thesis, consistent with the thesis of *The Acting Person*, that good men who choose not to stand up to Soviet evil represent a failure of the human act. Reagan drove home the thought:

It was C. S. Lewis who, in his unforgettable *Screwtape Letters*, wrote: "The greatest evil is not done now in those sordid 'dens of crime' that Dickens loved to paint. It is not even done in concentration camps and labor camps. In those we see its final result. But it is conceived and ordered (moved, seconded, carried and minuted) in clear, carpeted, warmed, and well-lighted offices, by quiet men with white collars and cut fingernails and smooth-shaven cheeks who do not need to raise their voice."

Well, because these "quiet men" do not "raise their voices," because they sometimes speak in soothing tones of brotherhood and peace, because, like other dictators before them, they're always making "their final territorial demand," some would have us accept them at their word and accommodate ourselves to their aggressive impulses. But if history teaches anything, it teaches that simple-minded appeasement or wishful thinking about our adversaries is folly. It means the betrayal of our past, the squandering of our freedom.

So, I urge you to speak out against those who would place the United States in a position of military and moral inferiority. You know, I've always believed that old Screwtape reserved his best efforts for those of you in the church.... I urge you to beware the temptation of pride—the temptation of blithely declaring yourselves above it all and label both sides equally at fault, to ignore the facts of history and the aggressive impulses of an evil empire, to simply call the arms race a giant misunderstanding and thereby remove yourself from the struggle between right and wrong and good and evil.

Ronald Reagan refused to be a quiet man. He raised his voice. He chose to act. He made a moral choice to resist the beast.

This was, for Reagan, part of a moral crusade against the evil of Soviet Communism.

John O'Sullivan points to the importance of Reagan's moral rhetoric: "He tells people that it really is an Evil Empire. There is no getting away from it." Reagan had captured "what no one else was quite verbally capturing, or expressing, and at least not at that level." He realized and expressed the "sickness in Communism," that it was "run on the basis of thuggery."

O'Sullivan recalls the case of Vladimir Bukovsky, who escaped the USSR in the late 1970s: "Bukovsky gives his first press conference, and somebody says to him, 'How many political prisoners remain in the Soviet Union?' And he replies, '280 million. Everybody in the Soviet Union is a political prisoner. The guard who kept me in prison, he was a political prisoner because he had to deny the truth. They all have to obey a lie.'" Reagan saw Bukovsky's statement, O'Sullivan notes, and he responded to it. Finally, a Western statesman spoke the truth, and in a way people could understand. The most effective form of counterpropaganda, O'Sullivan says, is "to tell people a truth they already know and which they recognize in your description."

This was Ronald Reagan's unique Cold War stagecraft. And few bravado performances conveyed it like the one in Florida on March 8, 1983, before that audience of evangelicals.

"When he calls the Soviet Union an Evil Empire," says Douglas Brinkley, "it was a big deal, even in Catholicism. That was, in its own way, a religious language on the international stage. Reagan got roundly beat up in America, particularly by secular people, but also by liberals, for using inflammatory language, calling a country an Evil Empire. But Reagan persisted."

He also stood apart from predecessors who never dared use such bold language. Reagan biographer Craig Shirley says: "He was one of the few Americans, one of the few national political leaders, who was calling them out and saying what they were, which was an Evil Empire. Nixon never called them an Evil Empire. Lyndon Johnson never did. Jimmy Carter kissed Leonid Brezhnev after the conclusion of SALT II!"

Once again, Pope John Paul II would have agreed with every word Reagan said.

Here were two former actors acting out morally—choosing good over evil—on the grand stage. Both realized how crucial their choices were in the high-stakes drama of the Cold War.

ACT II

3

ENTRANCES

Ronald Reagan and John Paul II each had a plan to act out. But could these charismatic characters, born a decade and a continent apart, ever be written into the same play? Most playwrights would not bother trying.

Looking back, however, we see surprisingly similar plotlines in the story of their lives.

It is striking to hear both men describe their idyllic hometowns and upbringing so similarly, despite so many differences in their lives.

"All of us have a place to go back to," Ronald Reagan wrote in his first autobiography. "Dixon is that place for me. There was the life that has shaped my body and mind for all the years to come after."[1]

"It was here, in this town of Wadowice, that it all began," said John Paul II. "My life began. And school began, my studies began, and theater began, and priesthood began.... As they say, there is no place like home."[2]

Both were born the second boys of two-child families. In a time when families were often large, theirs were small and tight-knit. Both mothers suffered major health problems when Ronald and Karol were eight years old. Karol's mom died from her illness.

Reagan's mother nearly died during the 1919 influenza epidemic, but she survived to live an abundant life.

Reagan and Wojtyła led physically active lives from boyhood. In high school, Reagan participated in football, basketball, and track, and he swam and played football in college. He later became an avid horseman. Wojtyła excelled at swimming, hiking, running, and soccer. His soccer league had teams of Catholics and Jews. Wojtyła was the only Catholic boy on the Jewish squad. He played goalkeeper.

As young men, Wojtyła and Reagan shared a mission to protect, even save, others.

For Reagan, this was a day-to-day operation during his seven summers as a lifeguard patrolling the Lowell Park beach at the Rock River in Dixon, Illinois, where he was on duty seven days a week. During those seven years, ages fifteen to twenty-two, Reagan saved the lives of seventy-seven people, which he tallied on a nearby tree stump. Those rescues became fundamental to his being and his mission.

"Sometimes people would express skepticism over the number of saves," says Reagan biographer H. W. Brands. "They would say, 'Reagan, you were a good-looking young guy and certainly those pretty girls who were thrashing around in the water, they probably weren't going to die.'" But Brands says that Reagan did not see a lot of humor in that: "He thought this was really serious business. And he would remember the seventy-seven notches [in the tree stump]. It was important to Reagan that he had rescued those people, and he didn't want to question the validity of those rescues. Reagan saw himself in some way or other as somebody who can come to the rescue of other people."

A young Wojtyła likewise strove to protect people's lives. He and his countrymen faced a threat far graver and all-encompassing: totalitarianism.

On September 1, 1939, when Wojtyła was nineteen, the Nazis invaded Poland from the west. Less than three weeks later, on September 17, the Soviets invaded Poland from the east. The inva-

sions occurred soon after Adolf Hitler and Joseph Stalin concluded their secret "nonaggression" pact. World War II had begun, and Poland stood at the epicenter of the two tyrants' death pact. All of Poland came under occupation.

Karol Wojtyła joined the underground resistance.

FATHERS AND MOTHERS

Friends and acquaintances of Nelle Reagan routinely described her as a "saint." But Ronald Reagan's father was hardly an angel. Jack Reagan suffered from what Nelle charitably told her boys was a "sickness"—a tendency to abuse alcohol.

When Ronald Reagan was eleven years old, he came home to the shocking sight of his father passed out on the front porch. Too drunk to have made it to the door, Jack Reagan lay exposed to the freezing February elements. The boy could smell the whiskey on his father's breath. "His arms were stretched out," Reagan later recalled, "as if he were crucified—as indeed he was." Reagan dragged his father into the house.

The young Karol Wojtyła's father was much more reliable. Here was a rock, of solid character and faith, a man who served in his nation's military and who was a faithful servant of the Catholic Church. Wojtyła's father was devout. He said his prayers and the rosary every day. Karol would for the rest of his life recite a prayer that his father wrote for him when he was a child:

> Holy Spirit, I ask you for the gift of Wisdom to better know You and Your divine perfections, for the gift of Understanding to clearly discern the spirit of the mysteries of the holy faith, for the gift of Counsel that I may live according to the principles of this faith, for the gift of Knowledge that I may look for counsel in You and that I may always find it in You, for the gift of Fortitude that no fear or earthly preoccupations would ever separate me from You, for the gift of Piety that I

may always serve Your Majesty with a filial love, for the gift
of the Fear of the Lord that I may dread sin, which offends
You, O my God.[3]

Pope John Paul II looked back at his father's home as his first
"domestic seminary."[4]

That is something Ronald Reagan would never have said about
his father, as much as he cared about his dad.

"His childhood was difficult for a young boy," says H. W.
Brands. "Reagan built this wall around himself because Jack Reagan,
who one day was the best buddy his son Dutch ever had, the
next day was drunk. He was unreliable. Reagan couldn't count on
him." Brands speculates that the moment Reagan encountered his
father sprawled in the snow was so devastating that he might have
momentarily considered leaving his father there. It scarred the boy.
Brands believes that to understand Reagan, one must understand
that he was the son of an alcoholic father. Such a father helped
spawn a certain aloofness in Reagan, Brands believes.[5]

Reagan said as much. His always-broke, pot-of-gold-searching,
shoe-salesman dad uprooted the young family at every turn. (Reagan
would live in thirty-seven different residences in his lifetime.[6])
Each relocation proved painful, and the little boy learned not to
bother making friends at a new stop. Reagan later conceded that
this nomadic life as a child probably made him "a little slow in
making friends." He added, "In some ways I think this reluctance
to get close to people never left me entirely."[7]

Reagan's daughter Patti put it this way: "He couldn't really *rely*
on his father."[8]

He thus turned to his Heavenly Father.

"I AM HIS OWN"

Not long after Reagan found his father passed out in the cold, he
asked to be baptized in his mother's church. Nelle introduced her

son to the pastor, the Reverend Ben Cleaver, who became a male role model to Reagan, one more stable than his own father. Reagan was baptized in June 1922, receiving permission earlier than most young people in the congregation.[9]

James Rosebush is one of the few Reagan advisers whose memoirs captured the significance of Reagan's faith. In several one-on-one conversations, Rosebush asked Reagan about his faith, and the president never hesitated to reveal his spiritual thinking.

Rosebush recounts how the White House one day received a letter from a constituent asking whether the president had any favorite hymns. Knowing that this topic would be of special interest to Reagan, Rosebush headed up to the family quarters and said, "Mr. President, we received a letter from someone who wants to know if you have any favorite church hymns." Without hesitation, Reagan replied, "Oh yes," and then sang three hymns. The president knew them by heart.

"You can imagine being sung hymns by the president of the United States, what that was like," Rosebush says. "He didn't have the best voice, but he was so earnest about them and he sang them, and he knew every single word."

The choice of hymns was revealing. The first, which Reagan told Rosebush was his favorite, was "In the Garden." The president sang it in full.[10]

Rosebush afterward rushed back to his office and looked up the words, because he recalled that the hymn had been his father's favorite as well. "The refrain of this hymn describes to a tee precisely what I thought Reagan felt about himself," Rosebush observes. "The refrain goes, 'And he'll walk with me and he'll talk with me and he'll tell me I am his own.'"

Rosebush places those lyrics within the context of Reagan's upbringing. "Now remember, Reagan was seeking refuge growing up because he didn't have it with his dad and he was looking for ways to feel comfortable and comforted. So this hymn, 'I will tell you that you are my own,' he felt this comfort."

Rosebush continues:

So Reagan had this conscious capacity to feel that he was walking with God. Now, this is critically important to understand Reagan. People say about Reagan, *Well, he didn't have any friends, he didn't have any close associates, what was going on?* And this is also why the official biographer, Edmund Morris, who spent thousands of hours with the president, never really understood Ronald Reagan. He called him one of the strangest men he ever met. Well, how could you say that about Reagan? Well, Reagan wouldn't disclose himself. But he did in these unique situations that I had with him. So he's really saying to me, by singing this hymn, he's saying, "Jim, I have a walk with God." Now, I saw this not only in a mystical way. I saw that Reagan had this other side, that Reagan had this influence on him that was divine.... So he used this walk with God and he used this confidence that he gained by having this constant relationship with a higher power. He employed that for good, but he was always listening for that.

Reagan took this Heavenly Father as his own, from those days in Dixon all the way to his time in the White House.

The fathers of both Ronald Reagan and Karol Wojtyła prompted their boys to look upward to God. In Reagan's father's case, that was unintentional: his own faults led his son to turn to the Heavenly Father. By contrast, Wojtyła's father intently taught his boy to look to heaven. He also told him to look there for a mother—after young Karol's mother, Emilia, died when he was eight years old. The senior Karol took his son to shrines to the Virgin Mary, saying, "This now is your mother."[11]

His earthly mother was gone. Sadly, when Karol was twelve, his older brother died as well, a victim of a scarlet fever epidemic. Then Karol's earthly father left too soon as well. He died of a heart attack on February 18, 1941. "I'm all alone," young Karol told friends. "At twenty [years old] I've already lost all the people I've loved."[12]

Ronald Reagan lost his own father just two months later, on May 18, 1941 (coincidentally, Karol Wojtyła's twenty-first birthday). Jack died of heart failure at age fifty-seven.

"When he died so young," Reagan said many years later, "I blamed it at first on his problem with alcohol. Now I think his heart may have finally failed because of smoking. I'd always thought of Jack as a three-pack, one-match-a-day man: In the morning he'd use one match to light his first cigarette of the day, and from then on, he'd light the next one from the old one."[13]

Reagan said he felt desolate and empty, especially since Jack seemed finally to be settling down and redeeming his life. Nonetheless, at the funeral Reagan felt a peace come over him, as if he could hear Jack's voice calling out to offer comfort from the other side: "I'm okay and where I am it's very nice. Please don't be unhappy." Jack's son turned to his mom and told Nelle, "Jack is okay, and where he is he's very happy."[14]

It was classic Ronald Reagan. He found a glimmer of light amid the gloom. Surely, God would work everything for the good.

"Let Theater Be a Church"

In this same period, Karol Wojtyła and Ronald Reagan threw themselves into acting—Wojtyła in the theater, Reagan in Hollywood, where he established himself as a star.

Both men took up acting early. The future pope began at his high school in Wadowice, Poland, under the tutelage of Mieczysław Kotlarczyk. The history and theater teacher emerged as a profound influence in the young Wojtyła's life.

Kotlarczyk came at acting from the vantage of faith. He shaped Wojtyła's thinking on the power of the proclaimed word to the stage and also to history and to expressing deeper truths about God. Kotlarczyk's students referred to him as "a deep Christian believer" and "a man of one idea, the theater." The stage offered a means not only to personal "perfection" but also to "transmitting the Word of God." George Weigel deduced that, to Kotlarczyk, the actor's function was not unlike that of a priest via sacrament and word: to open the realm of transcendent truth through the tangible materials of this world.[15]

Karol Wojtyła discerned both purposes and vocations.

"Let theater be a church," Wojtyła later declared.[16] As a playwright, he sought just that. Theater and church became so intertwined for him that he could make a smooth transition from actor-playwright to priest. Kotlarczyk's early influence had something to do with that.

Italian scholar Rocco Buttiglione refers to Kotlarczyk as a "theorist of the theater of words." He describes how the director excelled at enlisting the "evocative power of words, which not only communicate a meaning but also elicit an emotion, at once both entirely subjective and entirely objective; it is the power through which speech is lived." The highest value is found in the "profound intimacy" between the speaker and those who listen—an intimacy the actor introduces.

Buttiglione connects these concepts to Wojtyła's reflections on consciousness, the person, the act, and the philosophical notions of phenomenology:

> The import of the performance, the plot, the communicative function in the usual sense are, of course, drastically reduced in this type of theater. What happens to consciousness is more emphasized than the events per se; the key thing is the way in which the objective reality is revealed in consciousness.... In a certain sense, [Wojtyła's] first initiation to phenomenology came about indirectly and outside of the orthodox philosophy, through the theory of theater and, above all, the existential experience of being an actor under Kotlarczyk's direction.... In any case, it is certain that Kotlarczyk understood the liturgical character of theatrical action, the way in which it revives the presence of a universal value which renews mundane existence, judging its falsity but at the same

time offering the possibility of entering into a new dimension and an unexpected authenticity.[17]

Ronald Reagan took up stage acting at Eureka College in the early 1930s. He loved it. An economics major, Reagan effectively majored in theater as well. Remarkably, he acted in fourteen plays during his four years (1929–1932) at Eureka.[18] He thrived on the reaction he received from his first audiences.

In a sense, however, one can trace his acting career back further. He began performing in his boyhood hometown of Dixon. Here again, he had formative experiences as a young man of faith at his mother's side.[19]

Nelle Reagan was a respected voice at her church and in her community, and she brought along her son as a partner and apprentice. She soon had her Ronnie, her pride and joy, doing recitations at the church and elsewhere. The local paper, the *Dixon Telegraph*, reported on these happenings. On May 6, 1920, the newspaper reported that nine-year-old Ronald recited "About Mother" at the church. A few weeks later, the June 3 edition reported on his recitation of "The Sad Dollar and the Glad Dollar," which preceded a separate reading by his mom. As part of the church ministry, mother and son did two-person performances for patients at local hospitals. At the Dixon State Hospital in 1922, Ronnie and Nelle "entertained the patients with a short and enjoyable program," reported the *Telegraph*, she with a banjo and he with "two entertaining readings."

This special mom-son ministry went off so well that the Dixon congregation permitted it to become a monthly outreach program to local patients.[20]

In short order, young Ronald was spreading his wings. The *Telegraph* of December 22, 1924, alerted readers that the thirteen-year-old would handle the role of "Jimmie" in the church's Christmas play, *The King's Birthday*.[21] He was a big hit. "Ronald Reagan convulsed the audience by his one-act dramatic reading," reported the *Telegraph*'s impressed reviewer.[22]

Mom and son took their show on the road, traveling to other churches to do performances, such as the Disciples of Christ church in Tampico, the town where Reagan was born. A *Telegraph* reporter made the trip for that July 1925 performance, raving that "each number Mrs. Reagan gave was enthusiastically encored; Ronald Reagan was encored several times."[23]

Ronald Reagan learned his faith from his mom, his sense of God's Providence from his mom, his optimism from his mom, and even his acting from his mom.

"THE LIBERATING FORCE OF SUFFERING"

Theater became inseparable from Karol Wojtyła's resistance activities in occupied Poland. On more than one occasion, he and his fellow thespians hid Jewish friends from Nazi stormtroopers.

More than that, theater became a means of staking out and preserving Poland's national and spirituality identity. Wojtyła's country had been wiped off the map from 1795 to 1918. Now it faced extinction again. Hitler wanted it to disappear. In addition to Jews, the führer persecuted "the intellectual custodians of Polish language and tradition," in Buttiglione's words. On November 6, 1939, only weeks after the invasion, the Nazis arrested 183 professors at Poland's historic Jagiellonian University and sent them to a concentration camp.

Wojtyła was then a student at the university (where he would later serve as professor). Among other underground activities, he began clandestine studies. Secretly working with Jagiellonian professors in private homes, he and other students risked being detected, arrested, and sent to concentration camps.[24]

In 1941, Kotlarczyk, Wojtyła's old theater mentor, relocated from Wadowice to Kraków. He and his wife moved into Wojtyła's apartment.

There he decided to put his theory of theater into practice. But this would not be a mere theatrical exercise. Kotlarczyk saw drama as "a protest against the extermination of the Polish nation's culture on its own soil, a form of underground resistance movement against the Nazi Occupation."[25]

Wojtyła became a leading actor and writer in Kotlarczyk's underground troupe, known as the Rhapsodic Theater. The underground theater became, as Buttiglione puts it, a "form of national consciousness," in which individuals and communities rediscover "an essential steadfastness and persistent humanity in the face of the claims of power." Wojtyła and friends sought nothing less than to create (in Buttiglione's words) "the conditions for the survival and the growth of spiritual self-consciousness despite the lack of a genuine national state."[26]

Wojtyła wrote six plays altogether. Monika Jablonska, a Polish national and the author of *Wind from Heaven: John Paul II—The Poet Who Became Pope*, notes that through this work as playwright he not only revealed himself to the literary world but also conveyed the primacy of the spoken word in cultural resistance to the Nazi occupiers.

All his plays deal with the drama of human existence, and all were influenced by two major factors: Kotlarczyk's Rhapsodic Theater and the Romanticism of the father of Polish drama, the nineteenth-century poet Juliusz Słowacki.[27]

Jablonska believes that Wojtyła's work *Our God's Brother* represents "undoubtedly his masterpiece" and is crucial to understanding Wojtyła the man. Here he "contrasts most keenly" the attitude of the artist with the person of ethical-moral action (a precursor, in a way, to his philosophical notion of the Acting Person). This "political drama," as Jablonska calls it, recounts events from the life of Polish revolutionary Adam Chmielowski. But rather than taking the form of standard biographical drama, the play unfolds in the conscience of the protagonist. Chmielowski was a respected painter from Kraków who left his artistic career to serve Christ, most notably through a ministry to the poor. He became Brother Albert. This, Chmielowski believed, was a path toward "more freedom."

Wojtyła has his character conclude, "I know however for sure that I have chosen a greater freedom."[28]

Perhaps the most profound aspect of this drama is what it signals not about the subject but about the playwright. Jablonska and other Polish observers view the play as an expression of the "spiritual transformation" taking place within Wojtyła, as he transitioned from poet-playwright to philosopher-theologian and, ultimately, priest.[29]

Wojtyła wrote this play in the crucial period 1945–1950, beginning it during his final year in seminary in Kraków. During those years, Wojtyła and his countrymen experienced a great trial, as Poland transitioned from a Nazi-occupied to a Soviet Communist country. In the play, Wojtyła inserted these telling words: "Generally speaking, the essence of man is in his historical inexhaustibility. The extra-historical element is embedded in him; indeed, it is the very wellspring of his humanity. Any attempt to comprehend man implies reaching into the wellspring."[30]

Wojtyła worked through his suffering in his poems and plays. "I have lately given much thought to the liberating force of suffering," he wrote to Kotlarczyk on November 2, 1939, shortly after the joint German-Soviet incursions and divisions of Poland. "It is on suffering that Christ's system rests, beginning with the cross and ending with the smallest human torment."[31] Indeed, the Apostle Paul wrote at length about his suffering—how he had been flogged, lashed, beaten with rods, pelted with stones, shipwrecked, put in danger from rivers and bandits and Gentiles and fellow Jews and false believers. "I have labored and toiled and have often gone without sleep," he wrote. "I have known hunger and thirst and have often gone without food; I have been cold and naked." Paul had been "exposed to death again and again" (2 Corinthians 23–28).

Wojtyła, then still a student at Jagiellonian University, told Kotlarczyk: "I have written a new drama, Greek in form, Christian in spirit, eternal in substance, like *Everyman*. A drama about suffering: *Job*. Some people here quite like it. It is partly the result of my reading of the Old Testament. I have reread David's Psalms, the Book of Job, the Book of Wisdom, now the Prophets."[32]

Wojtyła's *Job* was a retelling of the Old Testament saga, and at the same time it embodied the sense of suffering and martyrdom of Wojtyła's Poland at that moment.[33] "The Lord gave, and the Lord has taken away, blessed be the name of the Lord," Job says in the Old Testament. "As for me, I would seek God, and to God would I commit my cause, who does great things and unsearchable, marvelous things without number."

Wojtyła wrote these words in *Job*:

In what I say I see one thing...
How souls are struggling with grief
Whether they are righteous or sinful....
I look and see: He is Harmony. I look and see: He balances
    all.[34]

Here we see a glimmer of hope from a man who, as pope, would describe himself as a "witness to hope." The message he conveyed in that passage from *Job* is not unlike Ronald Reagan's endlessly optimistic "God's Plan" theology: the loving Father would work out things for the best. Only in God, not in men, was there ultimate harmony and understanding.

Through God's Plan, the playwright would, decades later, become the first Slavic pope—a development that the great Polish poet Juliusz Słowacki had predicted in his prophetic 1848 poem, *Papież Słowiański* (*Slavic Pope*):

In the middle of the battle God will ring a vast bell.
For a Slavic Pope
He has also prepared a throne.
Listen, a Slavic Pope will come,
A brother of the people.[35]

God would ring that bell. That brother would come.

DARK NIGHTS OF THE SOUL

Around the time Wojtyła's father died, another crucial male figure entered the young man's life: Jan Tyranowski. As the Nazis rounded up Catholic priests, it fell to lay leaders like Tyranowski to continue clandestine ministry. From his apartment, Tyranowski led a "Living Rosary" group of teenagers and young adults. Karol Wojtyła joined the group. The devout teacher became a spiritual mentor to the future pope.

As Buttiglione notes, it was probably through Tyranowski's influence that Wojtyła chose to do his doctorate in theology on Saint John of the Cross, the sixteenth-century Carmelite friar.[36] Carmelite spirituality forever shaped Wojtyła, who identified with Saint John of the Cross and the great mystic's *Dark Night of the Soul.* He sought to learn Spanish solely to read the poem in its original language.

Saint John of the Cross, also known as Saint John of Avila, urged Christians to carry the cross with great strength. "If the Lord wants to lead us by paths of desolation and wants us to hear the painful language of which we are speaking, we should not be discouraged by anything that he sends," he wrote. "Rather, we should drink with patience the cup that the Father gives us, because he gives it, and we should ask him for strength that our weakness may obey him."

This must be done in order to meet God's will. "We should try, with the strength God gives us, to conform ourselves to his holy will obediently and quietly, and not to follow our own.... Beg the Lord that he open our eyes so that we may see more clearly than we see the light of the sun, that the things of the earth and the heavens are too base to desire and rejoice in, if they separate us from God's will."[37]

Saint John of the Cross insisted that we accept whatever level of sacrifice and suffering that comes as part of the Divine Plan: "There is nothing, however small and bitter it may be, that is not of great value if it is in accord with the Lord's will. It is incomparably more valuable to live with hardships if the Lord commands it than to be in heaven without his willing it."[38]

It is hardly a surprise that Wojtyła latched on to Saint John of the Cross during this time. With his father and mother having died, and his only brother as well, and with totalitarians ravaging his friends and his beloved homeland, his soul was enduring a dark night.

Still, throughout, he felt God speaking to him. As C. S. Lewis would later write, "God whispers to us in our pleasures, speaks in our conscience, but shouts in our pain: it is his megaphone to rouse a deaf world."[39]

Ronald Reagan listened for God's whispers as he experienced his own dark nights of the soul.

After moving so frequently in his early years, he was pleased when the family settled in Dixon for several years. He found stability at long last in the girl he thought was the love of his life, Margaret "Mugs" Cleaver. She was the daughter of the Reverend Ben Cleaver, Reagan's spiritual mentor and probably somewhat of a surrogate father.[40] Reagan saw, in his relationship with Mugs and in his hometown of Dixon, the simple, decent, homespun, Americana kind of life he wanted. He was sure that Mugs would be his wife one day, but she had other plans. She left him at Eureka College. The young Reagan was left brokenhearted.

Reagan's next love was the actress Jane Wyman. They married in 1940. He was devastated when he and Jane lost their daughter, Christine, shortly after birth, in 1947. In June of that year came a health scare that kept him in bed for weeks. He developed acute viral pneumonia—so threatening that biographer Edmund Morris said he "lay fighting for life" and "very nearly died."[41] Reagan was heartbroken again the next year when Jane filed for divorce. It was a divorce he did not want. He considered it a major personal failure. After Jane's spurning came the slow and painful deterioration of his movie career.

After the divorce, a bewildered and lonely Reagan entered his wilderness years. Gossip columnists and biographers have maintained that a lost Reagan—no longer Nelle's boy at the church in Dixon—began hopping into bed with various Hollywood starlets. How much of the accounts of womanizing is true remains unclear, but Reagan surely was searching for romance, love, or maybe the pleasure of escape. He was a bachelor, a free man, though not truly free. He was lonely and unhappy. With his marriage over and his career faltering, the path once seemingly laid straight before him had taken unexpected twists.

Then he met Nancy Davis. She became the real love of his life, reciprocating his dedication and fidelity.

The relationship took time, however. He and Nancy went on a number of dates after they met in late 1949, but then Reagan pulled back. Nancy later explained: "Ronnie was in no hurry to make a commitment. He had been burned in his first marriage, and the pain went deep." Even after their courtship resumed, Reagan held off on proposing. He asked her to marry him only after she decided to "give things a push," as she later put it: she told him she was thinking of going to New York to work in theater.[42] They married in 1952.

Ronald Reagan would be the first to say that the traumas and challenges he faced paled in comparison to those that Karol Wojtyła endured. But his struggles were undeniable.

And yet he almost always spoke fondly of his upbringing. He cherished the America that he learned about from his patriotic mother, from his storytelling father, from his pastor, from the American Legion, from the YMCA, and from the serene world of the early twentieth-century Midwest.[43]

"The beliefs that Reagan kept with him were ones that I would call all-American Main Street values," says Douglas Brinkley. "He really did believe in the Kiwanis Club, Rotary Club, Boy Scouts of America, college debate society, football on a local level, horseback riding." He believed in "localized democratic traditions" as the basis of Americanism. "Some people will ridicule Reagan as being a Hallmark president," Brinkley notes, "[but] he really liked the Fourth of July parade, the community pulling together with

4H clubs and high school alumni competitions, beauty pageants—these sort of Norman Rockwell–esque American aspects of the townhall-meeting feeling. Reagan really admired this, and he thought this was democracy at its best."

As Brinkley discerns, Reagan, a voice for freedom and democracy, "found democracy in his childhood growing up in the Great Depression and seeing how the communities of America in the Midwest pulled together and survived that economic maelstrom." He imbibed the America celebrated and taught in schools in those days—the McGuffey Reader, the old-fashioned civics classes. "And why wouldn't he believe them?" Brinkley asks. "It got him all the way to the White House two times, and he's one of the most beloved presidents in American history."

CONFRONTING EVIL

On the surface, Ronald Reagan and Pope John Paul II seem a most unlikely pair—Protestant president, Midwest, Eureka College, Hollywood versus the head of the Roman Catholic Church, Polish philosopher-theologian, raised in the crucible of totalitarianism in Eastern Europe. But look closer and the similarities quickly emerge.

Douglas Brinkley calls Reagan and John Paul II "kindred spirits." The historian notes some clear parallels: "both were underestimated," he says, "because they were handsome, because they were actors, because they were in some ways communicators—a lot of intellectuals didn't see them as heavyweights."

Beyond the parallels between their upbringings and experiences, and how outsiders misread them, Reagan and John Paul II displayed kinship in their views on human nature, on theology, on history, even on many aspects of politics.

Most important for the partnership they would form in the 1980s, they both understood that there was undeniable evil in the world that they needed to resist.

Karol Wojtyła experienced the evil firsthand. During World War II, he witnessed many Jewish friends and defiant priests condemned under the Nazis. Poland lost 20 percent of its population in the war, the highest percentage of any nation. More Jews lived in Poland than in any other country in Europe.

And then, almost as soon as the Nazis had been defeated, a different totalitarian threat subjugated Poland.

Bishop Robert Barron reminds us: "I think one of the most extraordinary things about the life of John Paul II was that he found himself between the pincers of the two worst totalitarianisms of the twentieth century. So first the Nazis with all their extraordinary brutality, but then there was a very brief hiatus and then in come the Communists."

The February 1945 Yalta Agreement, struck by the United States, Britain, and their wartime ally the Soviet Union, helped place Eastern Europe in Stalin's hands. Pulitzer Prize winner Anne Applebaum, an expert on the Soviet bloc, explains: "The Yalta Agreement was in essence the West's agreement to allow the Soviet Union to occupy Central Europe. There may have been some Americans who had some illusions that that was not what was going to happen after the war, but in practice that is what happened. The Soviet Union was allowed to enter those countries, and once it had entered them, it began immediately to change their political and economic systems." The Soviets implemented "Communist ideology" in "all aspects" of Eastern European life: the school system, the culture, independent institutions, independent trade unions, independent universities. "Yalta very much leads to totalitarianism or the attempt to create totalitarianism," Applebaum says.

Winston Churchill signed the agreement along with Franklin Roosevelt. Churchill learned soon enough that his efforts at Yalta represented a failure. One year later, in March 1946, he delivered his Iron Curtain speech in Fulton, Missouri, warning that international Communism posed a threat to Western civilization—to "Christian civilization," as he put it.

Most observers did not see the threat as clearly as Churchill did. But both Karol Wojtyła and Ronald Reagan recognized the atrocities that the Soviet Union would unleash on Eastern Europe. They also saw well before others that the Soviet empire—that Evil Empire—could not endure. Brinkley points out that Reagan was "predicting the breakup of the Soviet Union when no other intellectual of stature" believed that dissolution to be possible. Likewise, "Pope John Paul II is forecasting the end of Communism because it is godless."

The Nazis and World War II were gone, but the Soviets and the Cold War had arrived.

4

TRANSITIONS

The postwar world brought pivotal changes for the future pope and for the future president. Karol Wojtyła was ordained a priest in November 1946. He continued responding to his religious calling through the 1950s and 1960s as he transitioned from priest to bishop and finally to cardinal. Wojtyła saw himself as doing God's will. Here was his "DP."

Like Karol Wojtyła, Ronald Reagan was a young man in transition. He had left the tranquil confines of Dixon and Eureka College to head west. In California, he would find his way in film, in television, in politics.

Was this Reagan's "DP"? On its face it seems silly to see God's hand in *Knute Rockne, All American* or the Screen Actors Guild or *General Electric Theater.*

And yet that is exactly how Reagan interpreted matters. It is remarkable to look back and see how, through it all, he remained attuned to and confident in a Divine Plan. He could not always make out where the path was leading him, but he remained convinced that the plan would become clear in time.

This was still Nelle Reagan's boy. God still had a plan. Reagan was sure of it.

Reagan's Battleground

Reagan got his break in Hollywood in 1937 and found success early. By 1939 he had already appeared in nineteen movies, and he would make fifty-three films altogether. But for all his success at the box office, most of Hollywood's stars knew him for what he did for them in the negotiating room.

From 1947 through 1959, Reagan found a new starring role: as president of the Screen Actors Guild. This was a contentious time in Hollywood, as many Americans worried about a significant Communist presence in the film industry and how the Soviets could exploit Hollywood for propaganda purposes.

Reagan still considered himself a dedicated FDR Democrat. As his interest in global affairs and matters of state grew, so too did his concerns about Communist influence. As he later recalled in his autobiography, by the 1940s American films dominated 95 percent of the world's movie screens, with an audience of "500,000,000 souls" worldwide. "Takeover of this enormous plant and its gradual transformation into a Communist gristmill was a grandiose idea," Reagan wrote. "It would have been a magnificent coup for our enemies.... The Communist plan for Hollywood was remarkably simple. It was merely to take over the motion picture business... [as] a grand world-wide propaganda base."[1]

Vladimir Lenin had stated plainly that "of all the arts, the most important for us is the cinema." The head of Lenin's and then Stalin's Soviet Comintern, Grigory Zinoviev, insisted that motion pictures "must become a mighty weapon of Communist propaganda and for the enlightening of the widest working masses." In March 1928, the Soviets held their first Party Conference on Cinema. They knew what a tremendous force a friendly Hollywood could be.

Within Hollywood, there were dedicated Soviet Communists and Communist Party USA members like screenwriters John Howard Lawson (CPUSA no. 47275) and Dalton Trumbo (CPUSA no. 47187). Like other Hollywood Ten members, both swore a loyalty oath "to rally the masses to defend the Soviet Union" and "to remain at all times a vigilant and firm defender of the Leninist line of the Party, the only line that ensures the triumph of Soviet Power in the United States." Both saluted the red flag.

Lawson, widely known as "Hollywood's commissar," offered advice for spreading Communist propaganda through the movies: "As a writer do not try to write an entire Communist picture, [but] try to get five minutes of Communist doctrine, five minutes of the party line in every script that you write."[2] Trumbo agreed. He said that "every screenwriter worth his salt wages the battle in his own way—a kind of literary guerrilla warfare." He insisted that to not exploit Hollywood films for this purpose was "tantamount to abandoning the struggle altogether."[3]

These were the battle lines that Reagan faced as head of Hollywood's largest actors' union. And a battle it was. When Reagan attempted to break a Hollywood picket line, a mob pelted his bus with rocks, shattering the glass. He was warned that acid would be splashed in his movie-star face. He received so many threats that he began sleeping with a Smith & Wesson. Reagan would always remember how his views solidified during that era. He recalled seven months of negotiating with Communists and Communist-influenced people who tried to control some of the Hollywood unions. As they negotiated, mobs rioted in front of studio gates and bombed homes.[4] He saw all this Communist activity as grinding "a great industry" (his words) to a halt.[5]

A NEW DOOR OPENS

Even as Reagan found love with Nancy and influence as Screen Actors Guild president, his movie career faltered. He was left to perform a vaudeville act in Las Vegas at the seemingly aptly named Last Frontier hotel.[6] This was far from the glimmering lights of Tinseltown.

But then another door opened: television.

In 1954 the production company MCA-TV asked Reagan to host a weekly anthology series on CBS, *General Electric Theater.* Biographers have typically portrayed Reagan's move from film to television as a demotion. TV was still a relatively new medium and didn't carry the same prestige or glamour as film. No doubt Reagan himself would have preferred to remain on the big screen.

As it turned out, however, his new TV career became a coup for Reagan—a saving grace. This was the era when television took off in America: in 1950 there were fewer than ten million TV sets in America; by the end of the decade there were nearly seventy million.[7] And Reagan's show immediately became a hit. By 1956, in fact, it had become the third-highest-rated program on television, behind only *I Love Lucy* and *The Ed Sullivan Show.*[8]

GE Theater was so widely watched that it made Reagan a household name in a way that his film career had not. The show, which ran for eight seasons, gave him star power that set him up well for the next stage of his career.

Here again Reagan found vindication for his sense that God worked all things for the best. According to Nancy Reagan, he never abandoned that core belief, even at his lowest points. For instance, he never considered the Vegas gig beneath him or let it get him down.

Nancy explained later: "He again got back to the deep belief that everything happens for a reason. Whatever happened to him, there was a reason for it."[9]

As there was for Nancy: Reagan chalked her up to the Divine Plan, too. "If ever God gave me evidence that He had a plan for me, it was the night He brought Nancy into my life," Reagan said.[10]

So the divorce that he did not want and that he suffered through for years ultimately led him to the love of his life. Likewise, the collapse of his movie career unexpectedly opened a door to major television success.

That success, in turn, would open another door.

A TIME FOR CHOOSING

GE Theater gave Ronald Reagan another stage to work from beyond the set. He had become a popular after-dinner speaker in Hollywood after World War II. But the GE job took his public speaking to an entirely new level. As Reagan chronicler Lou Cannon notes, "The contract required Reagan to spend 10 weeks a year touring GE plants, giving as many as 14 speeches a day."[11]

Reagan thus took on a new role: not simply actor, but actor *and* politician. His talents and interests made him extremely well suited for this position. After all, he had long displayed a keen interest in politics and world affairs. One reason Jane Wyman cited for divorcing him was that, as the *Los Angeles Times* reported in 1948, "she could not bring herself to display the interest he showed" in political issues.[12]

Now GE allowed him to pursue his passions and hone new skills. Cannon calls Reagan's time with GE an "unusual political apprenticeship." Reagan went further, referring to the experience as his eight-year "postgraduate course in political science."[13] The actor still identified as a New Deal Democrat when he started working with GE. His anti-Communism played a major role in his political conversion, but so did touring GE's 139 factories in forty states, meeting thousands of workers, and seeing the power of the free market up close. During this time he read thinkers ranging from Jefferson and Madison to Lenin and Sun Tzu to the great free-market economists Friedrich Hayek and Ludwig von Mises.[14]

He also developed what would become known simply as "The Speech."

After years on the road with GE refining a presentation that distilled his core convictions, Reagan finally let the American people hear "The Speech" on the night of October 27, 1964.

That evening, the former Democrat appeared before a national television audience to endorse Republican presidential nominee Barry Goldwater. The speech, formally known as "A Time for Choosing," zeroed in on the fight for freedom and against tyranny.

Reagan talked about the perils of Communism abroad and a "creeping socialism" and smothering statism at home.

In effect, this speech launched Ronald Reagan's twenty-five-year-long freedom mission.

Reagan reminded his millions of viewers of the America the Founders had created. He quoted a Democratic senator who had recently defined liberalism as "meeting the material needs of the masses through the full power of centralized government." To which Reagan responded: "'The full power of centralized government'—this was the very thing the Founding Fathers sought to minimize. They knew that governments don't control things. A government can't control the economy without controlling people. And they know when a government sets out to do that, it must use force and coercion to achieve its purpose. They also knew, those Founding Fathers, that outside of its legitimate functions, government does nothing as well or as economically as the private sector of the economy."

Reagan biographer Craig Shirley expands on this philosophy: "Reagan agreed with the framers and founders that the Judeo-Christian philosophy impelled man to go forward in the search for freedom. America was, as Jefferson said and as Lincoln said, always on a search for a more perfect union. The expansion of human freedom has always been the mission of the United States of America. Whether it was slavery or suffrage or other definitions of personal and human freedom, America has always expanded the realm of personal and human and private freedom."

Of course, the totalitarian state sought just the opposite. It looked to retract freedom. That was what Reagan wanted to counter. It was also what Karol Wojtyła wanted to counter.

Nearly twenty years earlier, Reagan had learned that those whom he had seen as political allies failed to recognize certain forms of totalitarianism. In the 1940s, the proud Democrat Ronald Reagan received enthusiastic applause from fellow Hollywood progressives whenever he denounced fascism on the speaking circuit. Then, in 1946, the Reverend Cleveland Kleihauer, pastor of the Hollywood Beverly Christian Church, reminded Reagan that the Nazis had been defeated and that another danger could replace it: Soviet Communism. "I think your speech would be even better," Dr. Kleihauer said, "if you also mentioned that if Communism ever looked like a threat, you'd be just as opposed to it as you are to fascism."

Reagan took Dr. Kleihauer's advice in his next speaking appearance. After torching the fascists, he added a new line: "I've talked about the continuing threat of fascism in the postwar world, but there's another 'ism,' Communism, and if I ever find evidence that Communism represents a threat to all that we believe in and stand for, I'll speak out just as harshly against Communism as I have fascism."

The applause stopped. Reagan exited the stage to dead silence.

The addition of a single line to his popular speech had turned him into a flop. Reagan had just learned something crucial: the progressive circles he traveled in were happy to denounce Nazism but did not want to hear a bad word about Communism. Decades later, after his presidency, Reagan thanked the Reverend Kleihauer for the "wake-up call."[15]

Like Karol Wojtyła, Reagan recognized Communism for what it was. Craig Shirley invokes the Orwellian state that both Reagan and Wojtyła stood against: "There was a famous scene from the novel *1984*. Winston Smith has finally been outed as a subversive. He is dragged away to Room 101. O'Brien, the agent of Big Brother, the agent of the state of Oceania, has beaten him mercilessly, has starved him, has ripped his teeth out, has reduced his humanness to nothing." Finally, O'Brien asks Smith the ultimate question: *Why does the state desire power?* The answer, Shirley says, is that the state desires power precisely *because the state desires power*—because it wants to run people's lives. "It's nothing other than naked, raw power," Shirley says. "That is what Stalinism was about, what Communism was about, what socialism was about. And that means, by definition, you can't have God because you have individuals worshiping something other than the state, and the state cannot tolerate people worshiping something other than the state."

Reagan emphasized the dangers of the state throughout "A Time for Choosing." He drew for his audience a sharp line of demarcation between freedom and tyranny. It was a matter of human dignity. In his concluding line, Reagan declared that "you and I have the ability and the dignity and the right to make our own decisions and determine our own destiny."

On this point, Karol Wojtyła agreed. Communist tyranny, especially its militant Marxist atheism, robbed people of their human dignity and tried to keep them from reaching for God.

REAGAN'S NEW STAGE

By the time "A Time for Choosing" ended, a new door had opened for Ronald Reagan. The actor, it was clear, could make the transition to politics. David Broder, the famous *Washington Post* political reporter, called Reagan's performance "the most successful political debut" since William Jennings Bryan's "Cross of Gold" speech in 1896.

Reagan pursued politics. "When Reagan's film career was winding down," biographer H. W. Brands notes, "he decided to go on to a new stage. He went into politics and eventually found the largest stage in the world by becoming president of the United States."

First came the governorship of California. The political newcomer won his gubernatorial bid in November 1966, crushing a popular incumbent, Pat Brown. Reagan won by a million votes and a margin of fifteen percentage points, taking fifty-five of fifty-eight counties.

Reagan did not hesitate to credit the DP.

In a 1968 interview with the magazine *Christian Life*, California's new governor affirmed: "I've always believed there is a certain divine scheme of things. I'm not quite able to explain how my election happened or why I'm here, apart from believing it is part of God's plan for me."[16]

Another 1968 article reported: "Some of those who have attended conferences in Sacramento in which the Governor is faced with a decision, report that Reagan's reference to 'God's will' or plan is very much a part of him. According to these sources, he frequently blurts out, after listening to the pros and cons of a proposal, 'If it's God's will, let's do it.'"[17]

Writing in the *Washington Post* in January 1968, David Broder reported that some Reagan staff—most notably those urging him to consider a presidential run that year—were struggling with Reagan's determination to leave everything in God's hands. "He is described by his associates as fatalistic almost to the point of naivete in his belief that events will order themselves," Broder wrote. He quoted a Republican colleague of Reagan: "Ron honestly believes that God will arrange things for the best. But some of the people who made him governor are willing to give God a hand in making him President, and they're not too happy with the slowdown."[18]

But Nelle Reagan's son had always trusted in God's plan for him, even when he endured what felt like dark nights of the soul. And so if the White House lay ahead, well, the light would eventually shine there—maybe not in 1968, but at some point.

Reagan did run for the presidency in 1968, but the bid seemed half-hearted at best. The 1976 campaign proved to be a different story. He threw himself into achieving something remarkable: to wrest the GOP's nomination from the incumbent president, Gerald Ford.

Could this be the starring role for which Ronald Reagan was destined? Well, it depended on what the Master Director wanted for him.

"I have to realize that whatever I do has meaning only if I ask that it serves His purpose," Reagan wrote to a friend at the time. He added of his presidential bid, "If the task I seek should be given me, I would pray only that I could perform it in a way that would serve God."[19]

It turned out not to be the role for him; the spotlight would not be his just yet. In a dramatic showdown at the Republican Convention in Kansas City on August 19, 1976, Reagan missed securing the party's nomination by only 117 votes. He lost the delegate count to Ford by a final score of 1187 to 1070.

The 1976 loss seemed traumatic for everyone but Reagan. His daughter Maureen said she cried for two days because she was "just devastated" by the loss: "I just couldn't stop." When she saw her father long after the loss, she remained downcast. "Are you still crying?" he asked her with a smile, trying to cheer her up. He explained to her his philosophy on the matter—really, his theology: "There's a reason for this. I don't know what it is. But there's a reason." He told her: "Everything happens for a reason.... If you just keep doing what you're doing, the path is going to open up and you'll see what it is you're supposed to do."[20]

Maureen's father had learned that gospel long ago from his mother back in Dixon.

Around the same time, Reagan wrote a letter to an old Dixon role model, Garland Waggoner. A few years Reagan's senior, Waggoner had been the hero of the Dixon High School football team as well as a fellow Disciples of Christ member. He now served as a pastor in Storrs, Connecticut. Reagan assured Waggoner that he and Nancy were at peace with themselves and were awaiting whatever God had in mind for them.[21]

He displayed striking serenity for a man who had gone through a devastating divorce, lost his father, lost a child, and lost his movie career. Despite any dips or detours, Reagan maintained a truly sunny optimism about the path ahead.

God apparently had a bigger role in mind for Ronald Reagan. And for Karol Wojtyła, too.

A major plot twist was in the works.

ACT III

5

"BE NOT AFRAID"

On October 16, 1978, the unthinkable happened. Karol Józef Wojtyła was chosen as the first non-Italian pope in 455 years and the first Slavic pope ever.

No one had foreseen a Slavic pope—no one except the poet Juliusz Słowacki, 130 years earlier. God rang a bell; He prepared the throne for a Polish pope.

The two leading candidates for pope had both been, of course, Italians—Cardinal Giovanni Benelli and Cardinal Giuseppe Siri. Benelli and Siri were destined for the papacy, or so it was said. And yet that apparently was not part of the Divine Plan.

"The significance of electing a Polish pope was, first of all, that it broke a monopoly that Italians had held on the papacy for four and a half centuries," biographer George Weigel says. "The Catholic Church is not noted for taking dramatic shifts, of course. This was certainly one of them. Secondly, to elect a pope from behind the Iron Curtain was a bold step. And particularly to elect a pope who was a very, very astute combatant in the battle between Communism and Catholicism that had raged in Central and Eastern Europe since the end of the Second World War was another bold step."

Ronald Reagan, like so many other Christians, must have

marveled at the conclave's decision to take a pope from the jaws of the Soviet Bloc.

And not just any Soviet Bloc country. Wojtyła's homeland had resisted the Marxist-Leninist assault on faith more successfully than any other Soviet satellite.

Anne Applebaum explains: "Of all the Central European countries that were Sovietized after the Second World War, the system worked most poorly and ineffectively in Poland, both because Poland had a long tradition going back a couple of centuries of resisting foreign occupation and because Poland had the Catholic Church, and the Church was both a kind of ideological or spiritual alternative to Communism. It offered it a different set of values, it offered a different set of ideas, it offered a different way of thinking about the world, and it also literally offered physical space where the opposition could meet."

During the late 1970s and 1980s, the Polish opposition met in the basements of churches. The Catholic Church had become a haven even for people who were not religious but who could venture into a church building for activities ranging from art shows to political meetings. "It was a kind of system within the system," Applebaum says. "It was a system of spaces and institutions inside the Communist state that were not part of the state. This was fairly unique to Poland. The church in most other parts of Central Europe had been either communized, infiltrated, [or] repressed in various ways. It didn't have the power that it had maintained in Poland."

This link between the Church and the Polish resistance went back far. It would prove crucial to Poland and to the direction of the Cold War.

No Coincidences

How did Karol Wojtyła become Pope John Paul II? Stephen Kotkin, Cold War historian and Princeton professor, marvels at how things could have gone differently at so many points along the way. "What if Pope John Paul I had lived and not passed away so quickly?" Kotkin asks, referring to the stunning death of Albino Luciani only thirty-three days into his papacy. "Moreover, in the selection to replace John Paul I, the two leading candidates, both Italian, deadlocked. In other words, neither yielded to the other, which meant that the cardinals began to search for a compromise candidate." These were all "contingencies," Kotkin says. "There could have been different outcomes."

In some ways it seemed remarkable that Wojtyła appeared at the conclave at all. As a clandestine seminarian during the Nazi occupation of Poland, he could have been whisked off to a concentration camp like so many other Polish religious figures, including heroes of his like Maximilian Kolbe. Weigel points out that "John Paul II was very, very aware that, like so many of his friends, he could have lost his life in a very random way during the Second World War." And in 1944 a German truck struck Wojtyła as he walked home from work. He made it to the hospital only because a German officer realized that the bloodied victim was still alive and commandeered a passing lumber truck to serve as an ambulance. Wojtyła spent two weeks in the hospital. That accident could have ended his life then and there, in his early twenties.

Reflecting on these contingencies, Kotkin says: "It wasn't preordained that when he was hit by the car during World War II that Karol Wojtyła, who became John Paul II, would survive. It wasn't preordained that John Paul I would die after thirty-three days. And on and on one could go with these contingencies. This doesn't mean that everything is an accident."

Remember the oft-repeated words of John Paul II: "In the designs of Providence there are no mere coincidences."

"They Are Terrified"

When the Catholic Church chose a pope from the officially atheist Soviet Bloc, the Soviet state press betrayed no alarm. Only three bland sentences appeared about Wojtyła's elevation: "Rome, Oct. 16 (Tass)—The election of the new head of the Roman Catholic Church was announced here. He is a Polish Cardinal, Archbishop of Kraków Karol Wojtyła. He took the name John Paul II."[1]

Behind the scenes at the Kremlin it was another story altogether. Yuri Andropov, head of the KGB in Moscow, exploded at the KGB chief in Warsaw: "How could you possibly allow the election of a citizen of a socialist country as pope?"[2] Although the Soviets still had an iron grip on Poland, they feared a loosening of that grip. Now-declassified reports reveal just how much they dreaded this Polish pope.

Craig Shirley characterizes the Soviet reaction to the new pope: "They're not just watching; they are terrified. The pope, John Paul II, is a dagger aimed right at the throat of the Soviet Union, because he encourages free thought and free expression and free religion."

Stephen Kotkin observes that Moscow's fear was "well placed." He continues: "The pope was not afraid to declare what his principles and values were. It's an alternative morality to Communism, and the Communists are deathly afraid of the power of this alternative value system." As bishop of Kraków, Wojtyła had been well known to Communist officials, including the secret police. So, Kotkin says, "by the time you get to the pope's return to Poland, the KGB is frightened out of its wits."

Kotkin notes the contrast between the new pope and the Soviet leadership. The Soviet regime had "ossified," he says. The leadership was "old and wheezing and dying of various diseases, like emphysema or kidney failure." Meanwhile, John Paul II, the former athlete and actor, was physically robust and dynamic. At fifty-eight, he was the youngest pope in more than a century.

In his very first homily as pope, on October 22, 1978, John Paul II made clear the approach he would take. He exhorted the faithful: "Be not afraid. Open the doors to Christ. Open them wide. Open the borders of states' economic and political systems."

Weigel says that this message "was both evangelical and, in the context of the time, a powerful challenge to a political power. It really was speaking truth to power in a striking and effective way."

The message was exactly what Moscow did not want to hear. It was a moral suasion based on the overwhelming force of faith. Moscow had tried to strangle religion, and this was the starkest signal yet of its failure.

"Shrewd dictators know that one of the first places you crack down on is religion," Cardinal Timothy Dolan reminds us, "especially in cultures where religion is the storehouse of wisdom and memory and poetry and literature." That certainly applied to Poland in 1978, with its unique combination of ethnic, national, literary, and religious history. Worse for Moscow, because this new pope had come up under a Communist regime, he knew Marxism well enough to refute it.

As Bishop Robert Barron puts it, "He understood the enemy from the inside." Barron offers a telling example: "When he went into the conclave of 1978 that elected him pope, they were allowed to bring in some reading material. What did he bring? Not the Bible, not Thomas Aquinas. He brought, they say, a Marxist philosophical journal."

Poland's Monsignor Jarek Cielecki captured the importance of the elevation of Pope John Paul II when he observed, "There, on Saint Peter's Square, when [Wojtyła] came out on that balcony— that was the end of Communism."[3]

VICTORY AT VICTORY SQUARE

Only eight months later, John Paul II challenged the Communists on their own terrain, which was actually *his* terrain.

John Paul II made his triumphant return to Poland on June 2, 1979. The Communists had been worried about a papal visit to Poland from the beginning. The night of Wojtyła's election, top Polish Communist officials had gathered to determine how to respond to the news. One official asked, "What if the new pope decides to visit Poland?"[4]

The Kremlin tried to block the trip. Poland's Communist Party boss, Edward Gierek, tried to tell the Kremlin that it would be impossible to stop Poland's most famous native son from coming home. Gierek pleaded with Soviet general secretary Leonid Brezhnev, "How could I not receive a Polish pope when the majority of my countrymen are Catholics?" Brezhnev replied, "Tell the Pope—he is a wise man—that he could announce publicly that he cannot come because he has taken ill." Gierek tried to tell his boss that this proposal would merely delay the inevitable, since the people would demand a rescheduling of the trip after the pope recovered from his "illness." Brezhnev lashed out at his Polish underling, telling him that his predecessor "was a better Communist [than you]!" Finally, reluctantly, the Soviet leader consented: "Well, do what you want, so long as you and your Party don't regret it later." He slammed down the phone.[5]

They would all regret it.

On June 2, the pope arrived in Victory Square at the entrance to Warsaw's Old City. Immense crowds greeted him along the cobblestoned streets, which were bordered with garlands of flowers. Though faithful Poles would not deign to equate their hometown hero with Christ, the scene inevitably reminded some of Jesus's entering Jerusalem with crowds greeting him, waving palm leaves. Jesus had entered Jerusalem on a donkey mocking Caesar; surely the choice of Victory Square was a thumb in the eye of the Soviet Union.

The experience moved the pope. At the sight of the Cathedral of Saint John, tears ran down his face. No one had seen Wojtyła cry since his father's death nearly four decades ago. To fully grasp why he was so moved, says George Weigel, "you have to understand the significance of Saint John's Cathedral in Warsaw for Polish memory and Polish identity. During the Warsaw Uprising in August 1944, an almost insanely heroic attempt to throw off the Nazi yoke before the Soviet Army arrived, there was fighting pew by pew inside Saint John's Cathedral, which was leveled and then rebuilt after the war."

During Mass in Victory Square, John Paul II said, "Together with you, I wish to sing a hymn of praise to Divine Providence, which enables me to be here as a pilgrim." He examined the mystery of Providence further: "Leaving myself aside at this point, I must nonetheless with all of you ask myself why, precisely in 1978, after so many centuries of a well-established tradition in this field, a son of the Polish nation, of the land of Poland, was called to the chair of Saint Peter. Christ demanded of Peter and of the other Apostles that they should be his 'witnesses in Jerusalem and in all Judea and Samaria and to the end of the earth' (Acts 1:8). Have we not the right, with reference to these words of Christ, to think that Poland has become nowadays the land of a particularly responsible witness?"

The pope had a message for his fellow countrymen—and for the Communist leaders in Warsaw and Moscow: "Christ cannot be kept out of the history of man in any part of the globe, at any longitude or latitude of geography. The exclusion of Christ from the history of man is an act against man."

The Polish pope went further: "There can be no just Europe without the independence of Poland marked on its map!" He urged respect for "the rights of man, indelibly inscribed in the inviolable rights of the people."[6]

Thousands of young Poles marked the end of the speech by raising little wooden crosses in the air. They chanted: "We want God! We want God."[7]

Over the next ten days, rapturous crowds cheered and bells rang as Poland's most famous citizen traveled the country. The pent-up religious feelings of a people living under a repressive, atheist regime exploded. Imagine a million people showing up for Mass to get in line for Holy Communion. The church bells tolled the beginning of the end of the Soviet empire.

"All of a sudden, people know they are not alone," John O'Sullivan says. "Of course, dictatorships always have to create in you the fear that you are alone, that no one will come to your assistance. But that cannot be the case if you have John Paul II addressing huge crowds."

Anne Applebaum agrees: "The most important impact the pope had when he first came to Poland in 1979 was the fact that he brought so many people together. Suddenly there were hundreds of thousands if not millions of people who saw one another." Until that point, Poles "had no idea that there were so many people who felt the same way." Now they looked around and said in awe, "Look how many of us are here!" And then to have a pope speaking in their language, insisting that they need not fear the Communist government, "that language was very moving to people," Applebaum says.

In seeing the overwhelming numbers greeting the pope, Poles realized that they were part of a vast group that yearned for faith and freedom.

"It Was Just a Miracle"

The effect on the ground was electric, as Polish historian Marek Jan Chodakiewicz remembers from his childhood. Marek is the only male member of his family in three centuries who was not sent to jail, to Auschwitz, or to Siberia, or who had not been wounded or killed on the battlefield. The women of his family were equally tough. Marek's grandmother was tortured by the Gestapo, the Soviet NKVD, and the Polish Communist secret police for being a part of the pro-Western underground and bravely resisting totalitarians, both Nazi and Communist.

"I come from a long line of freedom fighters, people who die for the cause," Chodakiewicz says. "So I was raised not afraid and I, when I was a child, would challenge my teachers. I would tell them things against Communism when I was twelve years old—when I was chucked out of school for the first time. I was stupid because I was young, but I could be brave because nothing bad had ever happened to me personally, even though horrible things happened to my family." Being fearless himself, the adolescent Chodakiewicz was shocked to observe the constant trepidation in people around him.

The Communists imposed that fear. Chodakiewicz was sixteen years old when the pope made his return home. "John Paul II was scheduled to make his first ever visit to Poland as pontiff," he remembers, "and we were told at school in May 1979, *don't go*." School officials told students that attending any of the rallies would be tantamount to cutting school. When that threat did not work, the teachers and administrators tried to scare students, Chodakiewicz remembers: "We were then told, don't even entertain a thought because it's going to be like Mexico. There will be a stampede like a bullfight, and they'll scrape you off the wall. My teacher told me that."

Chodakiewicz did not know this at the time, but Poland's Communist regime had sent a directive to schools instructing them how to talk about the papal visit. "The Pope is our enemy," the directive said. "Due to his uncommon skills and great sense of humor he is dangerous.... Besides, he goes for cheap gestures in his relations with the crowd, for instance, puts on a highlander's hat, shakes all hands, kisses children.... It is modeled on American presidential campaigns."[8]

Chodakiewicz did not listen to the warnings: "Of course, I cut school with a couple of friends. The weather was beautiful and what I saw was a million-strong crowd. The best behaved, the best self-policed mass of human beings I have ever encountered. It was simply incredible. There was kindness, which was publicly surprising because Communism also meant churlishness. There was love. There was expectation of a miracle, and the miracle came. A dude in a white suit and a little yarmulke, John Paul II. We loved it."

Chodakiewicz emphasizes that the fear he had noticed everywhere began to dissipate after John Paul II came to Poland and told his people, "Be not afraid." For Chodakiewicz and the millions of other Poles who saw the pope during that June 1979 trip, the pontiff's message of hope "was astonishing and incredible." He concludes, "It was just a miracle."

The 1970s had been "stultifying—everything was dirty, corrupt, disgusting, mendacious. The pope came and emboldened the freedom fighters by showing us a miracle of his pontificate by preaching love, human dignity, and strength."

Also watching as a young man was Radek Sikorski, who, three decades later, would become Poland's foreign minister. Sikorski is married to Anne Applebaum. She recounts his experience from June 1979: "My husband, who was a teenager at the time, remembers going to see one of the pope's Masses and climbing a tree and seeing a sea of people." To him, too, "this was incredible."

That was the direct experience of the witnesses. Then they went home and turned on state television.

The Communist media did everything possible to downplay the pope's visit. They narrowed the camera lens so as not to show the massive crowds. They also avoided showing young people and children, focusing instead on old ladies in babushkas—anything to undercut the energy, the dynamism, the excitement, the outpouring of faith and hope.

The ludicrously slanted media coverage outraged Poles. Both Chodakiewicz and Applebaum note that the Communists' trick backfired: it only fueled people's fervor. Here Poles could see a stark example of how the Communist regime lied to them.

By merely showing up in Poland, the Polish pope was exposing the lies of Communism. The former actor need not even open his mouth. It was about his presence.

Unfortunately for the Communists, he opened his mouth, too. And with his words, he showed his people that the Communists were no longer directing the show. They had lost control of their sham production.

Poles could not have been more inspired or joyously defiant of the Communist regime. John O'Sullivan worked in those days for Radio Free Europe/Radio Liberty. He recalls an incident involving a "bemused Western reporter" who interviewed a Pole on the scene:

"The reporter goes up to one of the rallies and asks a working-class guy, 'Why are you here?' And the Pole says, 'I came here to do glory to the mother of God and also to spite those bastards.'"

As O'Sullivan observes, one could not easily separate the religious from the political at this point. That was not necessarily because of anything this Polish pope had done but rather because the Communists had made everything political and ideological, including the spiritual. Marxist-Leninists used their political authority to try to crush religion. Pope John Paul II had not come in the name of a political cause; he merely came to testify to the truth.

It was a truth the Communists had labored so long to suppress. John Paul II exhorted his people to acknowledge that Christ—not the state—was Lord. "If Jesus is Lord," says New Testament scholar N. T. Wright, "Caesar is not."

The pope did not call on the Poles to take up arms against the Communists. He did not need to. "John Paul II was a man of great prudence," George Weigel says. "He understood that his office was one in which power was moral power. He didn't deploy armies, he didn't have an air force, he didn't have a navy. But what he had was a megaphone. He had a great megaphone and he could preach human rights and the defense of the dignity of the human person in a way that Communist censorship could not block. And he could do that as no one else could because he was the pope."

John Paul II's comments—and his very presence—had revolutionary implications behind the Iron Curtain. But he did not stoke the crowd. In fact, he sought to calm them. John O'Sullivan recounts: "At one point, John Paul II is addressing a large group of young people who have gathered outside the hotel where he is staying, and they are singing songs and hymns, and he comes out and he encourages them. Eventually, he says, 'Now, let's all quiet down. It's late. Everybody, I would like you all to go back to your homes quietly.'" It was no accident, then, that Marek Jan Chodakiewicz saw such a well-behaved, "self-policed mass of human beings" around the pope.

O'Sullivan draws a subtle but important distinction between the approaches of the future partners John Paul II and Ronald Reagan. The pope, he says, "is not asking anyone to tear anything down." John Paul II surely saw that a peaceful spiritual revolution could undermine the Communists' violent political revolution. And as his partner Reagan began working on the political front, their joint efforts would have an extraordinary impact.

The Communists were panicked for good reason. The pope's people, and people throughout Eastern Europe, were inspired more than ever to tear the Iron Curtain apart.

6

THE PAPAL STAGE AND THE PRESIDENTIAL STAGE

As Karol Wojtyła took the world stage, his performance skills proved instrumental, if not vital, to the success of his efforts. He understood the symbolic importance of choosing Victory Square for his debut back in Poland—the right stage for the occasion. But even then, the right stage needs the right actor to carry home the performance. And John Paul II, former actor, did it spectacularly in Poland—as he would throughout his papacy.

"The key thing about Pope John Paul II," Douglas Brinkley observes, "beyond being a very handsome matinee idol type in his younger days—he had a following of people that really believed in his career as a thespian—by 1979 in Poland, he is generating just massive crowds. It is the most exciting moment to hit the Vatican in centuries.... But he always knows that he is communicating larger messages to pilgrims all over the world."

Brinkley draws an analogy to "the Protestant tradition here in America with Billy Graham Crusades, where fifty thousand people come to be told that Christ cares and loves you and that you can be saved." And yet, Brinkley adds, "Pope John Paul II was operating in a much more difficult situation. He's operating in Cold War Eastern Europe. Anything he did is bound to get the dander up at the very least of the Kremlin. But he believes so much in his mission, and he was such a good and decent person, that anybody who met him, saw him, heard him, knew that he was a beacon of light, that he was somebody who was a positive force...operating in a zone of darkness. And so he became kinetic. He developed box-office fans."

His fan base extended well beyond Poland. "People all over the world started wanting to meet, touch, see Pope John Paul II," Brinkley says. In the United States, the pope "became a phenomenon," especially in cities with "big Polish-American populations" like Chicago, Milwaukee, and Cleveland. "All over the country, but distinctly in the Midwest, he became a folk-hero pope," Brinkley notes.

Among those in the American audience was a future president.

"The Pope Is the Key"

Six thousand miles from Warsaw, another former actor looked on the pope's Victory Square performance with admiration.

From his home in California, Ronald Reagan watched TV footage of the pope's visit to Poland. Richard V. Allen, his friend and foreign policy adviser, sat with him watching the news report—which, unlike that of the Communist-controlled media, showed the massive, joyous crowds greeting the pope.

Allen recalls that Reagan was "astounded by the crowd size and was deeply moved by the outpouring of emotion." He vividly describes the scene he witnessed in Reagan's home on June 2, 1979:

> It happened the day I was in California to see Governor Reagan. It turned out it was on that very day that Pope John Paul II, newly inaugurated, visited Poland. I happened to be sitting in Reagan's study with him. We were having a discussion about something or other.... I turned on the television set in his study and there it was: the papal plane arriving and the pope descending the steps and kneeling down, as his first

action, to kiss the ground in Poland. That was amazing. It still chokes me up to speak of this moment. And I glanced over . . . at Governor Reagan, and I saw a tear in his eye. It was very, very interesting. It was the only time that I ever saw him tear up.

Allen adds that he teared up as well. But he notes an important distinction between himself and Reagan: "I'm a Roman Catholic. He was not." Still, the Catholic pope moved the Protestant Reagan deeply.

As he peered into the TV, Reagan leaned forward and declared that the new pope was "the key" to winning the Cold War. He immediately wanted to reach out to the new pope and the Vatican and "make them an ally." "Dick, that's it," Reagan said. "That's it."

The former California governor was still months away from announcing his candidacy for president. But then and there, he realized that John Paul II would be the crucial figure in determining the fate of Poland and, by extension, of the entire Soviet Bloc. Reagan immediately recognized that the pope's visit had planted a stake for freedom in the epicenter of the Communist world.

We have got to make them an ally. Reagan could now see the path ahead with clarity.

"Knock This Thing Down"

That game-changing moment in June 1979 occurred just months after Reagan had found renewed determination to fight Communism. Allen again served as eyewitness.

In November 1978, Reagan, Allen, their mutual friend Peter Hannaford, and their wives visited the Berlin Wall. The six of them entered East Berlin through Checkpoint Charlie and approached *Alexanderplatz*, a shopping plaza. They took in the scene. The contrast between the dynamic West and the depressed East struck all of them.

Just then, two East German Communist police stopped a citizen holding shopping bags. They used their machine guns to prod the man, forcing him to show his papers and reveal what he was carrying in the bags. Reagan had read extensively about the Communist assault on people's freedom, property, and dignity in accounts by the likes of Whittaker Chambers and Aleksandr Solzhenitsyn as well as in publications like *National Review* and *Human Events*. It was the sort of scene those who lived behind the Iron Curtain witnessed every day. But this marked the first time Reagan had observed this behavior firsthand.

The incident "set Ronald Reagan's blood to boiling," Allen has written. "Reagan was livid, and muttered that this was an outrage."[1]

Governor Reagan grew more outraged when he glimpsed the cement monstrosity itself: the Berlin Wall.

In his interview for this book, Allen recounted that day in Berlin in detail. It is worth quoting his words at length, as his recollection constitutes the fullest account of a key moment in the life of Ronald Reagan that influenced the direction of the Cold War:

> Berlin was behind the Iron Curtain. And from the American sector in Berlin, I took [Reagan] into the East. I took him to several notable places, parts of Berlin where he could see up close what it meant to live in Communist East Germany, one of the most repressive of all places in Eastern Europe. We went into an enormous plaza, a *platz*, as the Germans call it, and people were milling about and walking around.
>
> And he was just gathering the flavor of everything. Then I nudged him and told him to look over there. Two East German police, the *Volkspolizei*, were stopping a man who was carrying two shopping bags. One of them poked the barrel of his automatic rifle into the stomach of the man, and the other one probed with his rifle in the shopping bags to see what was in them. It was all I could do to restrain Reagan from going over and doing whatever he was going to do. I was afraid he

might punch the East German policeman. Then we'd really be in a pickle, wouldn't we?

I had seen this many, many times before. I lived in Berlin in 1960 before it was divided. I knew the city very well, so I knew that *platz* would be interesting. We took [Reagan] into a store, an East German store, to see the difference between an East German store and a West German store just a mile away. And then on the way to meet Axel Springer, Germany's largest publisher, [who] published newspapers and magazines like *Der Spiegel*, we stopped outside Springer's office, which had deliberately been built right up against the wall just a few feet away. [At that] very spot, a young East German [had tried] to escape through the barbed wire before the wall was built, and did not succeed. [He] was shot and left to bleed to death right there, calling for his mother. And Reagan wanted to visit that spot because I had told him about it.

So we stood outside, and that was his first direct encounter with the wall as such. As we approached the wall very close, just a few feet away, with Peter Hannaford and his wife on the left, and I and my wife, Pat, on the right, he stared at the wall, glowered, his jaw tightened, and he turned to me and said, "Dick, we've got to find a way to knock this thing down."

A really historic quote. I'll never forget it because, of course, then as president, nine years later, he would stand there and say, "Mr. Gorbachev, tear down this wall."

"Dick, we've got to find a way to knock this thing down." That, of course, was the thought that never left him.

In a way, the Berlin Wall still has not left Reagan. Not even fifty feet from his tomb at the Reagan Library today stands the largest chunk of the Berlin Wall outside of Germany. The free people of a free Berlin donated it to the memory and legacy of Ronald Reagan.

"WE WIN AND THEY LOSE"

Standing before the Berlin Wall that day in 1978, Dick Allen realized that Reagan's statement about the need to "knock this thing
down" revealed not only disgust but also intent. "I believe the
encounter with the wall and witnessing the armed harassment of
an ordinary citizen seared into the governor's memory the brutality of the communist system," Allen has written. It "reinforced his
dedication to placing it upon the ash heap of history." Allen added,
"It was clear from his reaction that he was determined to one day
go about removing such a system."[2]

So the experience in Berlin strengthened Reagan's determination to take down Communism. But Allen knew that the former
governor had already seen the need to challenge the Soviet empire.

In January 1977, Allen traveled to California to meet with
Reagan. Allen, then forty-one, was contemplating a run for governor of New Jersey and sought the former California governor's
endorsement.

But world affairs consumed their conversation instead. Only
days earlier, Democrat Jimmy Carter had been inaugurated as
president, having defeated the incumbent president, Gerald Ford,
from whom Reagan had nearly claimed the Republican Party's
nomination the previous summer. Allen recalls that they spent
about four hours "talking and talking and talking" about foreign
policy.

But Allen most remembers a bold five-word declaration Reagan made.

Deep into the conversation, Reagan looked Allen in the eye
and said: "Dick, my idea of American policy toward the Soviet
Union is simple, and some would say simplistic. It is this: We win
and they lose. What do you think of that?"

Allen had started his career as a graduate school researcher
for academics in prestigious universities like Notre Dame and in
respected think tanks like the Hoover Institution at Stanford, the
Center for Strategic and International Studies, the Council on For-

eign Relations, and the American Enterprise Institute. Some of his bosses in these institutions had been stalwart anti-Communists, but none—nor anyone at the government level, including the Nixon administration, where he served as an adviser—had shown such resolve toward Moscow.

Allen was stunned—and thrilled. The word *win* just didn't come up in discussions of the Cold War. "One had never heard such words from the lips of a major political figure," Allen has written. "Until then, we had thought only in terms of 'managing' the relationship with the Soviet Union. Reagan went right to the heart of the matter.... He believed we could outdistance the Soviets and cause them to withdraw from the Cold War, or perhaps even collapse."

Allen asked, "Governor, do you mean that?"

Reagan replied: "Of course I do. I just said it, didn't I?"

Allen paused and responded: "Well, Governor, I don't know if you ever intend to run again for president of the United States, but if you do, please count me in."

Reagan would do just that.[3]

"I needed no additional information," Allen recalled. "Herein lay the great difference, back in early 1977, between Ronald Reagan and every other politician: He literally believed that we could win, and was prepared to carry this message to the nation as the intellectual foundation of his presidency."[4]

But saying these things was one thing; finding a way to accomplish them was quite another. So when, two years later, Reagan watched Pope John Paul II in Warsaw, he recognized that they had a game changer on their hands.

Reagan wrote and recorded a radio broadcast reacting to the new pope's visit to Poland. He noted that Stalin had once mockingly asked, "How many divisions does the pope have?" Well, responded Reagan, that question had been answered: "Wherever [the pope] went in his native land the people of Poland came forth in unbelievable numbers. There were crowds of 400,000, 500,000, 1 million, and then 5 million, gathered from miles around." Reagan trenchantly asked: "Will the Kremlin ever be the same again? Will any of us for that matter?"[5]

Reagan, for one, was never the same again.

POLAND AS THE LINCHPIN

Watching the pope in Poland inspired Reagan. The moment suddenly opened new possibilities.

"I think when he first saw Pope John Paul II speaking in Poland," James Rosebush says, "he was infused with a degree of enthusiasm, an inspiration that was beyond what I think he even expected. He saw in the pope someone that he could not only just work with, because I think *work with* is sort of a mechanical term or a policy term, but Reagan, remember, always wanted to establish relationships with other people who he felt could further his mission, so you have to think of Reagan having a lifelong mission. This wasn't just for his time in the White House, but this was something he wanted to accomplish for mankind for all time, and he talked about it in those terms."

For all time: Rosebush remembers the force of these three words from Reagan. The president sought not a temporary shift in the balance of power but a permanent change that would bring freedom to the hundreds of millions of people suffering under Communism. And in the pope, Reagan recognized someone who shared his priorities, according to Rosebush. "'For all time,' he would say, and in seeing what John Paul was bringing to the table, it wasn't just John Paul's position at the time in the church, it was the spirit with which the pope thought, moved, and inspired people. And when Reagan saw the inspiration that the pope brought to the people of Poland, he thought this is an opportunity to make a compact with someone with whom [he] shared values and a commitment."

A chance for a major impact—for all time. Reagan saw an opportunity to change the world. And as Rosebush notes, one of

Reagan's favorite quotations came from Thomas Paine: *We have it within our power to begin the world over again.*

Reagan understood that Karol Wojtyła offered a fresh voice reminding the world that people had inalienable rights that came not from the state but from God. Reagan echoed this message. He also saw the courage in the new pontiff, who had resisted two totalitarian regimes.

Best of all, John Paul II came from Poland. As close Reagan adviser Bill Clark later said, "Reagan knew Poland would be the linchpin in the dissolution of the Soviet empire."[6]

Not everyone saw it that way.

In an editorial published June 5, 1979, the *New York Times* said, "As much as the visit of Pope John Paul II to Poland must reinvigorate and re-inspire the Roman Catholic Church in Poland, it does not threaten the political order of the nation or of Eastern Europe."[7]

Ronald Reagan begged to differ.

So did Moscow. The Soviets knew that the Polish pope had changed the game.

"What's interesting is that the Soviets were closer to the truth than the *New York Times*," Craig Shirley says.

Not everyone was as blind as the *Times*. Lech Wałęsa, whose Solidarity movement was in its infancy in Poland, said of the pope's almost messianic effect: "He comes to Poland and the twenty who followed me were suddenly ten million. It was a greater multiplication than the loaves and the fishes."[8]

And the situation was about to get much worse for the Kremlin.

THE PRESIDENTIAL STAGE

On November 4, 1980, Ronald Reagan was elected president of the United States. He won forty-four of fifty states against an incumbent president, sweeping the Electoral College 489 to 49.

Once Reagan took office the following January, Moscow faced virulently anti-Communist foes in both the Oval Office and the

Chair of Saint Peter. This was the last thing the Kremlin had expected only a few years earlier.

"Both of these men came to their high offices unexpectedly," George Weigel says. "No one in 1960 expected that Ronald Reagan would be president twenty years later. Hollywood actors simply didn't become president." Just as, Weigel adds, no one expected in October 1978 that John Paul II would be elected pope. Polish priests simply didn't become pope.

Weigel points out another important parallel: "Both of these men came to office with the sense of purpose, with a sense of vocational drive. They shared a conviction that Communism in Europe could be defeated without massive violence. That's an extraordinary conviction to share, and it had a real impact on history."

Reagan and John Paul II had reached the pinnacle of their careers. "Pope John Paul becomes the head of Catholics worldwide," Craig Shirley observes. "There is no more quest for power because he has already achieved the ultimate position of power inside the Catholic Church. Ronald Reagan is the fortieth president of the United States at age sixty-nine. There is no place to go that is more powerful. And both of them achieve these positions toward the last quarter of their lives. There are no more battles to win. Now it's just about the mission. And that tends to clarify the mind and sharpen the focus."

As Shirley notes, the two leaders had a shared focus: to defeat Soviet Communism.

REAGAN'S TURN

John Paul II had taken the world stage first, and everyone watched his captivating performance. Now Reagan entered, stage right, and this ex-actor also knew how to thrive in his role.

H. W. Brands observes how Reagan's previous careers prepared him for the presidency. Why did Reagan became the Great Communicator—the best at giving speeches in modern American political history, according to Brands? "He understood the power of speech. He understood the power of performing. It wasn't just the words. It was the way he delivered. It was the facial expressions. Kind of the nod and the smile. He knew how to tell a joke. He knew how to loosen an audience." Reagan knew how to win people over, Brands notes.

Douglas Brinkley agrees. He points to a respected C-SPAN presidential poll that he helps conduct, in which historians rank presidents along certain categories. When it comes to communication, "everybody" gives Reagan a 10 on a scale of 1 to 10, Brinkley says: "Even if you don't like Reagan's philosophy of conservatism, you have to give him a 10 at the way he could break through the glass and talk directly to the American people."

Reagan's years on the speaking circuit had strengthened these talents. But he first developed them as an actor, especially on TV. Brands argues that Reagan performed far better on television than on film, partly because he typically played himself on TV. (Reagan introduced and emceed every broadcast of *GE Theater*; he also acted in many of the episodes.) "When he was on the movie screen he was expected to play somebody else," Brands says, "and the somebody else he couldn't warm up to the way he could warm up to himself. [On television] he could just sort of be his own personality."

Reagan's quarter century in films and on TV prepared him for the "performance aspect" of politics, Brands maintains. The theater alone would not have given him the requisite experience. "Reagan was an expert at knowing when the camera was on," Brands says. "Reagan was an expert at knowing to never get caught making a bad face. You cannot find a bad photograph of Ronald Reagan. Part of it is he simply is a photogenic guy, but he always knew where the cameras were. He always knew when he was on." The historian adds that movie and TV actors need to be constantly aware of the cameras: "They have to know where to stand. They have to know about the lighting. They have to know how to hit their marks.... Reagan had to know how to convey his emotions, his message to a camera."

These would be enormously helpful traits in the age of the TV presidency. A hundred years earlier, most voters neither knew nor cared what President James Garfield looked like. In the second half of the twentieth century, the presidency increasingly became a celebrity role, where knowing how to act and how to communicate took on greater importance.

"Successful politicians understand that political office is a kind of dramatic role," Brands says. "Ronald Reagan knew this very well. It's not enough to master policies. You have to be able to sell your message. He understood instinctively that the most powerful tool in the arsenal of a president is the ability to inspire people. No president of modern American history was better than Reagan at communicating a particular vision of the United States and of the world."

Brinkley points to these attributes as well. Reagan learned a lot about communicating from his first political idol, FDR, who mastered radio as a means of connecting with the American people. But "Reagan adopted TV as his great tool," Brinkley says. "He knew the power of TV." Reagan had seen how John F. Kennedy used the power of television, and as a politician he made good use of TV, too. Brinkley recalls that Robert F. Kennedy had thought he could easily defeat Reagan during a nationally televised May 1967 debate, but instead "Reagan killed him because he knew how to use the soundbite, how to look right on television, how to seem like a leader."

Once Reagan became president, "he perfected how to give the moving speech." Brinkley recalls how Reagan incorporated the stories of everyday people into his State of the Union addresses to create "an amazing visual." The historian continues: "When we had dark moments, like when the *Challenger* blew up, Reagan knew how to talk to our national sorrows to be the grief counselor in chief. When we were figuring out a way to get over the malaise of the Vietnam War...Reagan decided to say, well, *it's morning again in America, let's go back to the World War II generation.*" Brinkley cites the June 6, 1984, speech at Omaha Beach in Normandy, where Reagan gave the extremely moving "Boys of Pointe du Hoc" speech. That speech did not merely honor those who fought at D-Day; it also served as a rallying cry about the need to defeat Communism. The president said that although America had liberated half of Europe during World War II, another half, Eastern Europe, remained to be liberated. *We did it then and we can do it again.*

"These were powerful rhetorical moments," Brinkley says. Reagan maximized the impact of his oratory by leveraging television: he timed major speeches like the Normandy address with key appearances on TV shows back home like *Good Morning America* and *Today* to "hit that morning audience with these kinds of feel-good American patriotic speeches," Brinkley notes. The result? "And suddenly, an entire generation of Americans that considered themselves Truman Democrats or Social Security Democrats, older Americans, abandoned the Democratic Party and went with Ronald Reagan because he was speaking their language of patriotism and the power of the American flag and American greatness, American exceptionalism, the City on the Hill. So this all was a performance by Ronald Reagan, but it was coming from being an astute observer of how to use the communication tools at the moment for [his] disposal."

Here Brinkley links Reagan and John Paul II through their shared experience as actors. The ability to "move audiences" comes out of "being an actor." Both men, Brinkley says, were always keenly aware of "playing to the crowd." They knew how to flourish on the "biggest performance stage of all."

Reagan and John Paul II had both mastered another skill: the ability to nail their live performances in one take, without a do-over. Brinkley discusses how this talent served Reagan especially well: "Performance, and a lot of presidential leadership, is done in real time. They are not paying a ticket to see you. So you have to be raw and real. The public has a great barometer. They can read somebody they don't like. They can notice a twitch or a bead of perspiration or a sigh. And Reagan knew that the cameras were always on and that it was capturing him." Reagan thus "took great advantage, always knowing that the mic was hot and being able to use communications in the 1980s like nobody else had done before."

TWO ACTORS EMERGE AND CONVERGE

As these two ex-actors entered the world stage, they found themselves acting in a big drama—a high-noon showdown with guys in black hats in Moscow. Here again, in this real-life morality play, Reagan and John Paul II put great stock not merely in saying their lines but also in making the right choices.

This was not a world of make-believe. They were moral actors.

As noted, George Weigel observes that both Reagan and John Paul II took from their theatrical experience "a view of life itself." And in their words and actions, they sought to convey their values.

Cardinal Timothy Dolan reinforces this point. "Ronald Reagan and John Paul II were able to portray their deepest values," Dolan says. "They would see acting not as an end in itself. They would see acting as a means to an end."

What was the end?

Dolan notes that some of both leaders' best performances centered on moral statements: "If you stand in front of the Berlin Wall and say, 'Mr. Gorbachev, tear down this wall,' that was great acting. When you are John Paul II and you take the bullets that had been removed from your body and then you bring them exactly a year later to the shrine of Mary, the mother of Jesus, at Fátima, and when you have them woven into her crown, that's acting in the best sense of the word. You are teaching the world something."

Note how one of Dolan's examples—John Paul II's bullet-in-the-crown moment at Fátima on May 13, 1982—involved no words at all. It was a silent gesture, but it could scarcely have been more poignant.

The best actors have presence. John Paul II and Ronald Reagan had it, and they put it on vivid display in the 1980s.

RESOLUTION

Any good production relies on more than the stage presence of the protagonist. Reagan did enough movies and *GE Theater* episodes to know that. Karol Wojtyła acted in and wrote enough dramas to know that.

As actors, Craig Shirley says, "both understood that a good script contains three essential elements: introduction, conflict, and resolution." Shirley elaborates: "They see themselves, as Shakespeare said, as players on a stage. The play is the thing, and they want to complete the narrative. They want to complete the story. They want to take what is on the stage and make it real for the people of the world. So they want to get through the resolution, and the resolution has to be the destruction of the Soviet Union."

They had come through the introduction already—their early years. Growing up under Hitler and then under Soviet domination shaped Karol Wojtyła's worldview; seeing the rise of increasingly restrictive government at home and totalitarian regimes abroad shaped Reagan's. Conflict emerged as they entered adulthood and forged ahead in their chosen fields: Wojtyła battled totalitarians from the 1940s through the 1970s, rising from resistance member to priest to bishop to cardinal; Reagan battled Communists in Hollywood and then fought for his principles in politics in the 1960s and 1970s.

Once the two men reached their positions of world leadership, they could look to the third part of the script: resolution. "And the resolution must end with a happy ending," Shirley says. "The story must end with a happy ending because they are both romantics. No doubt. You have to be. You can't believe in self-determination and not be a romantic."

But this story almost failed to reach a happy ending. Just weeks apart, the ringing of bullets nearly took out the protagonists.

7

THE BULLETS OF
SPRING 1981

Now we return to the scenes of the crimes in the spring of 1981: the Washington Hilton, only a mile and a half from Ronald Reagan's new home in the White House, and Saint Peter's Square, just outside Pope John Paul II's home in the Vatican.

In each crowd, a gunman awaits.

John Hinckley takes his shot first. On March 30, he stands outside the Hilton and fires his .22-caliber revolver at President Reagan. A .22 is a fairly small handgun, but Hinckley has loaded his weapon with bullets made to explode on impact.

One bullet ricochets off the president's armored car and slices into Reagan's body through his left armpit. It lodges in Reagan's lung, only centimeters from his heart.

Reacting swiftly, Secret Service agent Jerry Parr throws Reagan into the presidential limousine, which takes off right away. Parr, recognizing that Reagan has been shot, vetoes the plan to take Reagan back to the White House and tells the driver to go straight to George Washington University Hospital.

The snap decision saves the president's life.

The *New York Times* will report, on the testimony of the president's doctor, that the injury costs Reagan about 3.7 quarts of blood; the human body holds 5 to 6 quarts.[1]

BLEEDING TO DEATH

The second would-be assassin is Mehmet Ali Agca.

On May 13—only six weeks since Reagan's shooting—Agca stands in the crowd in Saint Peter's Square. John Paul II, riding in the back of his slow-moving Popemobile, waves to the huge crowd, occasionally shaking hands and kissing babies.

The twenty-three-year-old Agca carries a 9-millimeter semi-automatic. When the pope comes within a few yards of him, the trained assassin lifts the gun and fires four shots.

He finds his target.

John Paul II collapses. "Mary, my mother; Mary, my mother," he says.

The Popemobile races out of Saint Peter's Square, and security transfers the pope to an ambulance. Rome's traffic becomes almost impassable, but the ambulance finally makes it to Gemelli Hospital.

By now, the pope is barely conscious. He asks a nurse, "How could they do it?" Then he loses consciousness.

The situation looks dire. The hospital rushes the pope into the operating room. "Blood pressure 80, 70, still falling," a doctor calls out. John Paul II's heartbeat is barely detectable.

Father Dziwisz, who caught the pope in his arms after the shooting, gives last rites as the pontiff lies on the operating table.

The doctors begin emergency surgery. The chief surgeon finds "blood everywhere." The procedure will last some five hours as the doctors try desperately to stop the hemorrhaging and close multiple wounds.[2]

NEAR-DEATH EXPERIENCES

A mere six weeks separated these two assassination attempts. Both the president and the pope nearly died.

At the time, however, reports downplayed the severity of their injuries, largely because even their staffs did not understand how grave their conditions were. The official word from Washington suggested that Reagan remained in stable condition and that, in the words of the secretary of state just after the shooting, "there are no alert measures that are necessary at this time or contemplated."[3] Similarly, Vatican Radio reported that John Paul II was "not in serious condition." In reality, the pope's physicians still listed his condition as "critical" ten days after surgery.[4]

"We now know that both [shootings] were life-threatening," Cardinal Timothy Dolan says. "By the tiniest measurements available to human calculation, the bullets missed vital organs."

Dolan is right: Hinckley's bullet landed just short of Reagan's heart and nearly ruptured a valve. Agca's shot missed John Paul II's main abdominal artery by "the merest fraction of an inch," George Weigel reports. Just as remarkably, the bullet managed to miss the spinal column and every major nerve cluster along the way.[5] Even still, the pope's abdomen suffered so much damage that doctors had to remove nearly two feet of intestine.

In each case, a matter of mere centimeters made the difference between life and death. Both the pope and the president were fortunate not to have bled to death even before they reached the hospital.[6]

Once doctors began to attend to them, Reagan and John Paul II desperately needed blood transfusions. Reagan required eight pints of blood; John Paul II, six pints. After the pope's body rejected the first transfusion, doctors in the hospital donated their own blood.[7]

Both men came close to dying, only to survive and resume their positions of leadership. If you want to understand the depth of the bond they formed, you must look to the assassination attempts in the spring of 1981.

A WELL-TIMED JOKE

Although Hinckley nearly took Reagan's life, many people remember the assassination attempt for the sense of humor the president displayed.

Famously, before Reagan underwent emergency surgery, he said to the doctors and hospital staff, "I hope you're all Republicans." The entertainer in Reagan rose to the fore.

"Reagan, right up until the time he went under the general anesthetic, played the part," H. W. Brands observes. "He is joking as he goes into the operating room." Brands points out that Reagan had tried out the line earlier, when nobody was paying close enough attention for it to register. "So he tries it again... and that's when the head surgeon says, 'Well, today, Mr. President, we are all Republicans.' And that is the part that's remembered."

The ex-actor understood the role of humor in easing anxiety. Looking to calm a worried Nancy, he borrowed a line from the boxer Jack Dempsey and told his wife, "Honey, I forgot to duck."

"THE HAND OF GOD"

Ronald Reagan and John Paul II suffered strikingly similar near-death experiences. And they reacted to those experiences in strikingly similar ways.

Specifically, they both saw the hand of Heaven in their ultimate survival.

Before his surgery, as he struggled to breathe, Reagan cut the jokes and began to pray. "But," he later wrote in his diary, "I realized I couldn't ask for God's help while at the same time I felt hatred for the mixed up young man who had shot me. Isn't that the meaning of the lost sheep? We are all God's children and therefore equally beloved by him. I began to pray for his soul and that he would find his way back into the fold."[8]

After the surgery, Reagan "seriously began to think that there was some destiny here," according to Brands. "That there was some divine purpose. That God had spared him for a reason."

A number of sources have confirmed that Reagan expressed his certainty that God had intervened to save his life. Those sources include family members like his children Maureen and Michael, and close White House advisers like Bill Clark, Kenneth Duberstein, and Lyn Nofziger.[9]

Reagan's diary entry from April 11, the day he left the hospital, shows that he had the Divine Plan on his mind. He concluded the entry by writing, "Whatever happens now I owe my life to God and will try to serve him in every way I can."[10]

As Reagan recuperated in the White House, he began to consider how he might end the Cold War. Could halting the arms race with the Soviet Union be the special purpose for which he had been saved? Writing in his memoir years later, he recalled that moment of reflection: "Perhaps having come so close to death made me feel I should do whatever I could in the years God had given me to reduce the threat of nuclear war; perhaps there was a reason I had been spared."[11]

This sense of the Divine Plan inspired Reagan to take action. He wrote a long letter to Soviet general secretary Leonid Brezhnev. National Security Council and State Department staffers completely rewrote the president's message. At first the president seemed inclined to acquiesce, but then longtime aide Michael Deaver reminded Reagan that the American people had elected him, not some State Department bureaucrat, to be president.

Reagan agreed. "You know, since I've been shot," he told Deaver, "I think I'm going to rely more on my own instincts than other people's. There's a reason I've been saved."[12]

Reagan mailed his original letter. Even as he expressed his desire for negotiations between the two superpowers, he displayed the clarity of principle that had so impressed Dick Allen. "I must be frank in stating my view," he wrote Brezhnev, "that a great deal of the tension in the world today is due to Soviet actions." And in a handwritten cover letter, Reagan reminded the leader of the Soviet totalitarian empire, "Government exists for [people's] convenience, not the other way around."[13]

The president mailed that letter on April 24, only a week after Cardinal Terence Cooke, archbishop of New York, told Reagan, "The hand of God was upon you." That was the meeting in which

Reagan told the cardinal what he had previously confided to his diary: "I have decided that whatever time I have left is for Him."[14]

Not long thereafter, Mother Teresa reinforced the divine sense in President Reagan. During a private White House meeting on June 4, the nun told the president that she and her fellow Sisters of Charity had stayed up for two straight nights praying for him after his shooting. This comment humbled Reagan, but then Mother Teresa went further: "You have suffered the passion of the cross and have received grace. There is a purpose to this."

And what was the purpose of his suffering? "This has happened to you at this time because your country and the world need you."[15]

This statement moved Reagan; the Great Communicator remained speechless. Nancy Reagan cried.

James Rosebush witnessed the exchange. "I'll never forget the day," he says. "This saintly person told the president that she felt that his life had been spared for a specific purpose. And I could see that the president, it wasn't something that he took as praise. It was something that the president took as a confirmation for him, that he had a role in history to play and that it was based on his faith and that he had to, again, [take] that walk with God and God telling him what to do."

Mother Teresa's message must have made a particular impression on Reagan by virtue of *who* delivered it. Douglas Brinkley notes that "of all the people on the world stage," Reagan was "most impressed with" two. One was Pope John Paul II, "for the courage he exhibited in the belly of the beast of Eastern Europe when totalitarianism reigned supreme." The other was Mother Teresa. In *The Reagan Diaries*, which Brinkley edited, Reagan referred to her as "wonderful Mother Teresa," a "most remarkable little woman" who is "an inspiration" and "radiates joy because God, as she says, has given her the opportunity to serve the lepers, the poverty stricken & the hopeless."[16]

Think of the potency of Reagan's moment with Mother Teresa: "Because of your suffering and pain," the future saint informed him, "you will now understand the suffering and pain of the world."

That piercing reflection carried authority coming from a woman who daily witnessed immense suffering and pain in the world.

THE THIRD SECRET

Ronald Reagan had not fully recovered from his shooting when gunfire rang out in Saint Peter's Square on May 13, 1981.

The circumstances behind the assassination attempts differed. Reagan's shooter, John Hinckley, was a mentally ill young man who acted alone, operating under the delusion that he could impress Jodie Foster by killing the president of the United States. The pope's shooter, Mehmet Ali Agca, was a veteran terrorist, a paid assassin, "an exceptionally gifted killer used for exceptional assignments," as an Italian judge would later say. As we will see, Agca most certainly did *not* act alone.

Pope John Paul II, like Ronald Reagan six weeks earlier, almost immediately felt a powerful impulse to forgive. Before he lost consciousness, the pope told Father Dziwisz that he had forgiven his assailant.[17]

So close to death that he received last rites, John Paul II was, he later wrote, "already practically on the other side."[18] But he sensed that he would not cross all the way over. "At the very moment I fell," he said later, "I had this vivid presentiment that I should be saved."[19]

How and why had his life been spared? The pope's thoughts turned to these questions during his recovery.

He took special notice of the fact that the shooting had occurred on May 13, the feast day of Our Lady of Fátima—sixty-four years to the day after the first of six reported appearances by the Virgin Mary to three shepherd children in Portugal.

A word of explanation before we go any further here. We recognize that some readers will find odd, off-putting, or absurd the concept of the Virgin Mary's playing a role in a historical event like the assassination attempt on John Paul II. But we ask you to stick with us, even if you do not believe in the supernatural or if you are a religious person skeptical of Catholic claims of Marian apparitions. We do not aim to convince you of the Marian connection. Rather, we cannot omit the Virgin Mary from the story, for the simple reason that John Paul II himself believed devoutly that the Blessed Virgin "directs our daily journey on earth" and makes comprehensible "certain events" in "human history."[20] That included the attempt on his own life.[21]

Fátima carried special meaning for John Paul II because of his devotion to the Virgin Mary. That devotion began in childhood, after his mother died and his father said of the Blessed Virgin, "This now is your mother." John Paul II consecrated himself and his papacy to the Virgin Mary. His papal motto was *Totus Tuus*, which is Latin for "Totally Yours," meaning totally Mary's. Two decades after the shooting, in a 2003 Angelus address, the pope affirmed his commitment to "entrusting everything" to Mary.

After his shooting, the pope recalled the three prophecies the Blessed Mother had made at Fátima, which became known as the "secrets of Fátima."

The first two secrets were well known to Catholics. Mary predicted that the Great War, still raging in 1917, would soon end but that an even deadlier war would follow. She also warned, "Russia will spread its errors throughout the world, raising up wars and persecutions of the Church." This prophecy about the rise of atheistic Communism came three months before the Bolshevik Revolution.

But the Third Secret of Fátima remained a mystery. The Vatican had sealed it in a vault, where it stayed for decades.

Little wonder, then, that the pope thought of Mary and Fátima after his shooting on May 13. His aide Father Dziwisz later reported that John Paul II made the connection while still in the hospital: "He started reflecting on what was, to say the least, an extraordinary coincidence. Two thirteenths of May! One in 1917, when the Virgin of Fátima appeared for the first time, and one in 1981, when they tried to kill him. After pondering it for a while, the Pope finally requested to see the Third Secret."[22]

The Vatican delivered the Third Secret to the pope on July 18, 1981. What John Paul II read stunned him.

The secret involved a "bishop dressed in white." The only bishop who wears white is the bishop of Rome—that is, the pope. The three shepherd children who received the vision saw the pope "killed by a group of soldiers who fired bullets and arrows at him."

When John Paul II finished reading, Father Dziwisz said, "all his remaining doubts were gone." In this vision "he recognized his own destiny."[23]

The pontiff connected the secret to what had happened to him on May 13, 1981.

Of course, John Paul II did not die, as the bishop in white in the vision had died. But the pope did not see this as a reason to believe the assassination attempt had not fulfilled the Third Secret. Father Dziwisz explained: "Couldn't that have been the real point of the vision? Couldn't it have been trying to tell us that the paths of history, of human existence, are not necessarily fixed in advance? And that there is a Providence, a 'motherly hand,' which can intervene and cause a shooter, who is certain of hitting his target, to miss?"[24] Mehmet Ali Agca, a trained assassin firing at point-blank range, should have been "certain of hitting his target."

For reasons Dziwisz suggests, John Paul II became convinced that the Blessed Mother had interceded to deflect the bullet enough to save him.

"One hand fired," the pope remarked, "and another guided the bullet."[25]

John Paul II later said: "Could I forget that the event in Saint Peter's Square took place at the date and at the hour when the first appearance of the Mother of Christ to the poor little peasants has been remembered for over sixty years at Fátima in Portugal? For in everything that happened to me on that very day, I felt that extraordinary motherly protection and care, which turned out to be stronger than the deadly bullet."[26]

"A Higher Purpose"

After the assassination attempt on Reagan, John Paul II sent a message to the president, offering his prayers and best wishes for a full recovery. Reagan thanked the pope for the message and vowed: "My administration will continue to advance the goals which we both share. Please be assured of that."[27]

On the day of the pope's shooting, Reagan sent this brief message to John Paul II:

May 13, 1981

Your Holiness:

I have just received the shocking news of the attack on you. All Americans join me in hopes and prayers for your speedy recovery from the injuries you have suffered in the attack. Our prayers are with you.

Ronald Reagan[28]

Reagan did not merely observe diplomatic protocol when he sent this message. His concern ran deep. The leader whom he had identified two years earlier as the "key" ally to take on Communism now lay in a hospital, fighting for his life. National Security Adviser Dick Allen later wrote that Reagan asked him "every day for weeks thereafter about the pontiff's recovery." Allen said that "the president's affection for the pope was greatly magnified" by the shooting.[29]

Reagan conveyed that feeling in a note he wrote five days after the assassination attempt, on the pontiff's sixty-first birthday. To ensure that the pope received this special letter, the president asked the respected Italian-American congressman Peter Rodino, a New Jersey Democrat, to deliver the message personally.[30]

Reagan's note suggests the strong connection between the two leaders. In it the president wrote: "Happily, few leaders in the world today have the dubious distinction of knowing with some precision the kind of event you have just experienced. Fewer still can appreciate, as can I, the depth of courage and commitment on which you must have called, not only to survive that horrible event but to do so with such grace, nobility, and forgiveness."

Cardinal Dolan sees the Divine Plan in play here. He observes that the pope and the president became "convinced that there was some divine protection" involved in their surviving the assassination attempts. That shared conviction prompted them to engage in "serious examination about what God had in store for them now," since "He obviously was sparing them for a higher purpose."

Bishop Robert Barron expands on this idea. In his view, both Reagan and John Paul II were living in the grander theo-drama, in which one sees himself as responding to the prompting of God's will in living in service to others. In this model of the theater of life, man endeavors to go beyond the secular and the social, seeking a transcendence in which he also gains clarity about himself and his role in this world.[31]

To do so can mean to endure suffering, according to Barron. "Often those who bear the theo-drama participate in the cross in a very profound way," the bishop says. "Can I understand the full contours of that? No. Can I articulate it very clearly? No. But it seems to be a rule that those who are very implicated in the theo-drama become very implicated in suffering."

Bishop Barron says that John Paul II "would have read [his assassination attempt] as he read everything else—as part of the Divine Plan." Barron asks: "Did it give him a heightened sense of his mission to struggle against what he saw quite correctly as the supreme evil in the world of his time"—that is, atheistic Communism? "I would say, yes, absolutely. And again, that brings him close to Ronald Reagan."

The frightening events of spring 1981 pushed John Paul II and Reagan together. Bishop Barron concludes: "There is a very deep mystery we're touching on, which I think is Divine Providence.... It's one of the most intriguing parallels between them: They both understood that they were preserved through this suffering for a high purpose. And I don't think you'll understand either one of them without understanding that."

Accepting their personal sacrifices, the pope and the president prepared for the historical-spiritual mission ahead.

8

"HOW PROVIDENCE INTERVENED"

From the moment Karol Wojtyła became John Paul II, forces in the Soviet Union began working to vanquish this unusual pope. He posed too much of a threat to Moscow.

John Paul II, like Reagan, had the ability to turn a complex message into powerful symbols and words—and to move nations. He, like Reagan, could expose the underlying malevolence of an Evil Empire. The Kremlin had worried about John Paul II from the beginning, and their fears intensified with the pope's triumphant visit to Poland.

The stakes rose still higher with Ronald Reagan's electoral triumph in November 1980. Facing the one-two punch of an anti-Communist Vatican and anti-Communist White House, Soviet officials could hardly contain their anger. Already expert in agitation, propaganda, and incendiary rhetoric, the Communist press ratcheted up the vitriol directed at the occupant of the Chair of Saint Peter.

In the weeks between Reagan's January 1981 inauguration and the bullets of March and May, Moscow accused John Paul II's Vatican of being infested with "dyed-in-the-wool anti-Soviets and Nazi remnants." Imagine: Karol Wojtyła, survivor of the Nazi assault on Poland, a *Nazi remnant*.[1] Other wild aspersions followed, particularly aimed at what Moscow saw as the gravest of threats, a potential Reagan–John Paul II alliance. One Soviet publication called the pontiff "malicious, lowly, perfidious, and backward" and a "toady of the American militarists." This "toady" was waging battle against socialism with his "overseas accomplices," particularly his "new boss in the White House."[2]

Such vicious character assassination betrayed the Soviets' unmistakable fear that Washington and Rome could align against them.

The alliance that Moscow so feared was now materializing. After their near-death experiences, President Reagan and Pope John Paul II returned to work. Back in the Oval Office, the resilient Reagan was ready to speak out publicly in support of his ally in the Vatican and against his adversary in the Kremlin.

TRANSCENDING COMMUNISM

On May 17, 1981, only four days after the shooting of the pope, Reagan gave the commencement address at the University of Notre Dame. It was sheer coincidence that his first major public appearance after the terror perpetrated on the feast day of Our Lady of Fátima occurred at a Catholic university named for Our Lady. Then again, as John Paul II often said, in the designs of Providence, there are no mere coincidences.

Reagan seized the moment. He used the speech to proclaim his grand vision for the Cold War. Here, in what he would look back on as "one of the first major addresses of my presidency," he spoke almost as simply and directly about his approach to Soviet Communism as he had in a private conversation with Dick Allen back in January 1977. "The years ahead are great ones for our country, for the cause of freedom and the spread of civilization," Reagan said at Notre Dame. "The West won't contain Communism, it will transcend Communism.... It will dismiss it as some bizarre chapter in human history whose last pages are even now being written."

H. W. Brands notes what a change this kind of statement signaled. "Other American presidents tried to figure out how to *manage* the Cold War," he says. "Reagan wanted to *win* the Cold War."

Reagan then brought up John Paul II and the horrifying events in Saint Peter's Square four days earlier. After speaking of compassion, sacrifice, and endurance, the president observed the irony that "one who exemplifies [those traits] so well, Pope John Paul II, a man of peace and goodness, an inspiration to the world, would be struck by a bullet from a man towards whom he could only feel compassion and love."

Still speaking about the pope, Reagan returned to the larger theme of the address: the need to confront Communism. "It was John Paul II," he said, "who warned in last year's encyclical on mercy and justice [*Dives in Misericordia*] against certain economic theories that use the rhetoric of class struggle to justify injustice." Reagan then quoted what the pope wrote in that encyclical: "In the name of an alleged justice ... the neighbor is sometimes destroyed, killed, deprived of liberty, or stripped of fundamental human rights."

Reagan did not need to explain what he meant by "certain economic theories."

This passage is telling for another reason: it seems to telegraph Reagan's instinct that the Soviets played a role in what had transpired in Saint Peter's Square. Reagan didn't know it at the time, but his CIA director, Bill Casey, harbored similar suspicions. The morning after the pope's shooting, on May 14, Casey had called a meeting of the Foreign Intelligence Advisory Board to see whether he could ascertain what the Soviets were up to.[3] It was the first step in a long line of suspicion and inquiry from Reagan's intelligence chief.

In the Notre Dame speech, the president drew a sharp contrast between the free world and the Soviet empire: "For the West, for America, the time has come to dare to show to the world that our civilized ideas, our traditions, our values, are not—like the ideology and war machine of totalitarian societies—just a facade of strength. It is time for the world to know our intellectual and spiritual values are rooted in the source of all strength, a belief in a Supreme Being, and a law higher than our own."

Bishop Robert Barron remembers Reagan's Notre Dame speech well. In this address, the president critiqued what Barron calls the "failed Marxist presumption" that views humanity through a narrowly economic lens. Once we read mankind that way, Barron says, "we've divorced human beings from their rootedness in God." Barron argues that both Reagan and John Paul II "wanted to correct" such a flawed understanding of humanity. "A bad theology led to very bad anthropology," Barron remarks, "and that led to the disaster of the totalitarianisms of the twentieth century."

Taking on totalitarianism made the stakes supremely high. President Reagan conveyed those stakes in his May 17 address:

> History will ask—and our answer [will] determine the fate of freedom for a thousand years—Did a nation born of hope lose hope? Did a people forged by courage find courage wanting? Did a generation steeled by hard war and a harsh peace forsake honor at the moment of great climactic struggle for the human spirit?... The answers are to be found in the heritage left by generations of Americans before us. They stand in silent witness to what the world will soon know and history someday record: that in [its] third century, the American Nation came of age, affirmed its leadership of free men and women serving selflessly a vision of man with God, government for people, and humanity at peace.

"There's a reason I've been saved," Reagan had said privately. He was making sure the world knew it.

THE KREMLIN INADVERTENTLY FORGES A BOND

The Kremlin had feared a papal-presidential alliance. The assassination attempts could have derailed that alliance. But Reagan and

John Paul II survived, and their shared suffering "brought them closer together," as Bill Clark later said.[4] The attacks didn't forever separate the two leaders but instead forever united them.

Moscow suddenly had much *more* to fear.

Reagan's heightened interest in and affection for John Paul II quickly became clear. At the president's constant urging, Dick Allen brought Reagan updates on the pope's recovery "very frequently, three or four times a week," Allen says. And the president made sure to communicate with John Paul II. Throughout 1981, the president and the pope and their staffs frequently exchanged letters, cables, messages in diplomatic pouches, phone calls.

A memo from the end of that year, dated December 29, 1981, captures the flurry of activity. Writing to James Nance of the White House, Jim Rentschler of the National Security Council (NSC) expressed concern that there actually might be *too much* contact between the Reagan White House and John Paul II's Vatican: "We seem to be overloading the Vatican circuits of late," Rentschler wrote. Nance, responding on White House letterhead, conceded the "risk of overloading" but said that this "special consultation with the Holy See is warranted."[5]

Bill Clark replaced Dick Allen as national security adviser on January 1, 1982. He immediately noticed the frequency of the Washington-Rome dialogue. He and NSC aide Dennis Blair discussed the matter in memos dated January 5 and 8, 1982. "Messages have been flying back and forth between the White House and the Holy See on Poland," Blair wrote to Clark. Clark agreed that "we have been exchanging frequent messages with the Pope on the events in Poland," but, like Nance at the White House, he saw the ongoing correspondence as critical. It would continue. In fact, it would intensify.[6]

Of course, the general public knew none of this. These memos, telling as they are, remained confidential at the time. The Reagan Library did not declassify them until two decades later.

The fact that the public did not know all that was going on behind the scenes served a purpose for these two very public men.

As official Reagan biographer Edmund Morris observed: "Men of power mustn't give away their mystery. As long as you are mysterious you can move any way. Leaders who are secretive...do better than those who utterly reveal themselves. Reagan and the pope understood that."[7]

They knew when to keep the dialogue from public awareness and, conversely, when to let the world know they were conferring. Establishing a direct dialogue was something they very much wanted to do.

AT THE VATICAN: JUNE 7, 1982

The pope and the president finally got their chance to meet in person at the Vatican Library on June 7, 1982. They spent a lot of time together that special day, including almost an hour in one-on-one conversation.

It helped that the pope spoke English (among about a half-dozen languages). "So there wasn't an interpreter to slow things down," Craig Shirley says. They established a connection quickly.

Douglas Brinkley says that Reagan so honored John Paul II that the pope was "the one person that he was intimidated to meet." According to Brinkley, Reagan once said, "Mother Teresa and Pope John Paul II are the only two people I kind of get the butterflies to meet."[8]

Butterflies or not, Reagan hit it off with the pope. It probably helped that he had grown so accustomed to meeting and speaking with famous people. "I think the most important thing about Ronald Reagan," Brinkley says, "was that being famous for so long, being such a big Hollywood star, when you are hanging out with Charlton Heston or John Wayne or Bob Hope, you're not blown over by meeting a celebrity. When Ronald Reagan came to Washington in 1981, that Hollywood background meant a lot to him."

It helped, too, that Reagan had grown up around Catholics (his father and brother) and had Catholics all around him on his staff. Bill Clark often observed, "Ronald Reagan understood more about the Catholic Church than most Catholics I know."[9] Bob Reilly, who worked in the administration, said, "We considered Reagan an honorary Catholic."[10] Craig Shirley says that "Reagan was what I call a cultural Catholic." Shirley adds, "Reagan viewed the world differently than previous presidents because of his father's upbringing and because he was inculcated with what I call a parish perspective."

Reagan and John Paul II shared a common bond. As Cardinal Timothy Dolan notes, the two men were *"simpatico,* as the Italians would say." They connected, especially over the pope's Polish homeland and its vital importance in the global battle before them. The pope and the president both spoke to the paramount importance and interconnectedness of faith and freedom and the need to speak out against evil.

Above all, they looked each other in the eye and confided their mutual conviction that God had spared their lives a year earlier for the divine purpose of defeating the Communist empire. It was the president who invoked the hand of Providence, telling the pope, "Look how the evil forces were put in our way and how Providence intervened."

George Weigel, the pope's biographer, finds Reagan's comments striking. "I think that statement of President Reagan's to the pope demonstrates his own faith that God's Providence was at work in his life," Weigel says. "He certainly didn't expect to be instructing the pope on the reality of Divine Providence. He knew the pope knew that already. But it must have struck him, as I'm sure it struck John Paul II, that there was a certain curious, perhaps even providential symmetry in the fact that they had both survived assassination attempts within two months of each other."

Weigel adds that John Paul II had lived since his early twenties in the conviction that his life was being directed by God's purposes and that his task was to try to discern what those purposes were and then to bend his will to God's will. A similar conviction probably came to President Reagan "after he survived the assassination attempt in 1981," Weigel says. *"Why have I been spared? I have been spared for a purpose."* But by June 1982, "when these two considerable figures meet," theirs is a "meeting of men who both believe that they are called to live according to God's purposes for their lives." They pursued such a life by "discerning what is possible, what is doable, what is prudent, but also not settling for the world's notion of what can be done."

That last point is crucial. At a time when most observers thought that preserving the status quo represented the best hope for the Cold War, Reagan and John Paul II "shared a conviction that Communism in Europe could be defeated and could be defeated without massive violence," Weigel says. "That's an extraordinary conviction to share, and it had a real impact on history."

Cardinal Timothy Dolan likewise argues that Reagan and John Paul II bonded over their belief that they had been spared from death for this greater theo-historical purpose: "That innate, simple, yet sincere trust in Divine Providence brought them together. Here you have a man, Ronald Reagan, a man of deep faith who was raised in the Disciples of Christ tradition, . . . and John Paul II, who was extraordinarily fervent and devout, both of them would share that biblical view of reality and of history. And boy, I think there was a bond . . . that developed because of that."

Bill Clark confirmed that the bond was strong from the start. He later called June 7, 1982, a wonderfully "transformative" day, for it "gave the president and pope the ability to form a very personal relationship from then on." They both believed they had survived the attacks because God had saved them for a special mission—a "special role in the Divine Plan of life," Clark said. This would be, in Clark's estimation, the power of "The DP" unfolding.[11]

The pope and the president shared not only a bond and a sense of mission. They also united in seeing Poland as the wedge to crack the Communist Bloc.

During the Vatican meeting, the president invoked Poland in their shared mission: "Hope remains in Poland. We, working together, can keep it alive."[12]

Those must have been the sweetest of words to the Polish pope—a thrill to hear from a non-Polish (and non-Catholic) president.

As Carl Bernstein reported in a groundbreaking 1992 cover piece for *Time* magazine, during that first meeting both leaders expressed their conviction that a free, non-Communist Poland would be, in Bernstein's words, "a dagger to the heart of the Soviet empire." They were certain that if Poland became democratic, other Eastern European states would follow.[13]

Bernstein quoted a cardinal close to the pope: "Nobody believed the collapse of Communism would happen this fast or on this timetable. But in their first meeting, the Holy Father and the president committed themselves and the institutions of the Church and America to such a goal. And from that day, the focus was to bring it about in Poland."[14]

RESURRECTING THE "MARTYRED NATION OF POLAND"

It is fascinating to observe Ronald Reagan's heartfelt concern for Poland—a nation to which he had no ethnic connection. Reagan was Irish on his father's side and a blend of Irish-Scottish-English on his mother's side.

And yet he had a "preoccupation with Poland," said Bill Clark. "He had mentioned Yalta as far back as I go with him"—to the 1960s in California—"as being totally unfair and having to be undone someday."[15]

The Polish pope obviously felt the same way. Bernstein reported that both Reagan and John Paul II "refused to accept" how the Yalta Agreement had handed Eastern Europe over to Communist control, even though others viewed that division as "a fundamental political fact of their lifetimes." Reagan said of the pope and himself, "We both felt that a great mistake had been made at Yalta and something should be done."[16]

Reagan made his concerns for Poland evident in that first meeting with the pope and in his public remarks afterward. After their one-on-one in the Vatican Library, the pope and the president gave statements to the press together. In his, Reagan referred to "certain common experiences" that he and the pope "shared in our different walks of life," which had given their meeting "a special meaning for me." He gestured to the pope and pointed to "another special area of mutual concern," namely, "the martyred nation of Poland—your own homeland."

The *martyred* nation of Poland. It was indeed that. The Polish pontiff knew it; he had lived it. But he must have been surprised to see that the American president didn't shy away from expressing it before the international media. Similarly, he must have been moved to hear Reagan extol Poland as a "brave bastion of faith and freedom in the hearts of her courageous people, if not in those who rule her." Faith and freedom were Reagan's "twin beacons," and he knew the Communists repressed both in Poland.[17] After all, Poland's Communist regime had imposed martial law in December 1981.

Liberating the Polish people would mean supporting the Solidarity movement and stopping martial law. "We seek a process of reconciliation and reform that will lead to a new dawn of hope for the people of Poland," Reagan said, "and we'll continue to call for an end to martial law, for the freeing of all political prisoners." Reagan asserted that the Solidarity movement "speaks for the vast majority of Poles."

And now he and the Polish pope would speak for Poles from their respective stages.

Reagan would do that often in the months and years ahead. He appeared so often at Polish-American events and issued so many statements about Poland that an outraged Soviet propagandist at *Izvestia* complained, "One has the impression that it will not take much more for Reagan to start speaking fluent Polish!"[18]

The Soviets would not have liked what Reagan said at the Vatican that June 7, 1982. The president spoke of John Paul II's pontificate and the Holy See in general as "one of the world's greatest moral and spiritual forces" in a "troubled world...still stalked by the forces of evil."[19]

He and the pope, working together, would resist those forces of evil.

"The Same Level of Confidence in a Divine Power"

One of the few surviving witnesses close to Reagan and at the Vatican that day is James Rosebush. As deputy assistant to the president, he joined the official presidential entourage to Rome. Rosebush would rub shoulders with this pope three times, twice while accompanying the president and once with Nancy Reagan alone.

"That was the first time [of three times] that I was blessed by the pope," he says, "and I have to say that my own encounter with him was remarkable because he had an ability to hold your hand and look at you in your eyes with this piercing discernment and love that was indescribable for me, and I'm not even a Catholic."

To Rosebush, the pope and the president appeared to be operating from the same spiritual plane: "When that encounter occurred for me, I knew that the president was dealing with someone who was functioning on the same level, someone who had the degree of spiritual discernment that Reagan had as well, someone who knew that he had an hourly, minute, moment-by-moment walk with God." Rosebush says he came to understand Reagan better "through my meeting with the pope and being blessed by the pope." He explains: "It wasn't the ritual or the protocol of the moment—I have lots of pictures of us standing there in the audience with the pope, which was a wonderful and remarkable and historic moment—but that was when he took my hands, looked into my eyes, and blessed me, I thought, as Reagan said himself, *this is a person I can really work with.*"

Rosebush observes that Reagan felt a kinship with other leaders. For example, Reagan said something similar about Soviet leader Mikhail Gorbachev—namely, *this is a person I can work with.* And the president built an important relationship with Margaret Thatcher. But Rosebush believes that the kinship with John Paul II was entirely different, because it was a *spiritual* kinship: "The most important story to tell here is that Reagan and the pope were operating on the same level of spirituality, the same level of confidence in a divine power. This is what made this compact and this partnership even more powerful and productive."

Rosebush sees that June 1982 meeting as the opening act in their shared drama—one with a heavenly director: "I think the meeting between the president and the pope was a part of a Divine Plan." Recalling his front-row seat to this historic first meeting, Rosebush says, "You could see there was a delight on both faces." He believes both Reagan and John Paul II recognized that they had been called to this place at a time "appointed to them by a divine power." He knew that the Divine Plan "was something that Reagan lived by," and at the Vatican it became clear to Rosebush that the pope felt the same way. "Their life and their character was obviously infused by it," he says.

Rosebush pauses here to go where few have ventured. He notes that Reagan as a young man might well have gone to divinity school instead of majoring in economics at Eureka College. Indeed, many friends and congregation members expected him to become a pastor, because he was so advanced in his faith and active in church.[20] Rosebush believes that this background strengthened Reagan's connection to John Paul II: "I always say that if Ronald Reagan had gone to divinity school, he might have ministered to thousands of people in his lifetime, but he became an evangelist for freedom. So he was able to minister to millions of people, and the pope also brought his message of hope and freedom to millions of people. So the compact between the two of them, you could see that there was a great reverence for each other, a great respect, but also a sparkle in their eye that gave you a sense that they recognized the opportunity before them, the opportunity to work together and what they could accomplish."

That June 1982 meeting at the Vatican set them on their course.

THE PLAN UNFOLDS

That course took the form of "a de facto alliance between Reagan and John Paul II," John O'Sullivan says. Going into the 1982 meeting, the pope had suspected that Reagan desired peace, despite heated accusations that the president was a warmonger. The one-on-one confirmed John Paul II's instincts. O'Sullivan reports that the pope left that meeting telling two of his cardinals, including his secretary of state, "Reagan is a man of peace." Now he knew he could partner with the American president.

Although O'Sullivan describes the relationship between Reagan and John Paul II as an "alliance," he says he finds the term misleading and insufficient. The word *alliance* "implies a purely political arrangement," O'Sullivan says, one "intended to increase the power and influence in the world of any of the actors." By contrast, the pope and the president embarked on "a moral crusade," as they attempted "to create a better world for people." O'Sullivan explains: "Reagan is not just operating as a power-hungry American politician. He is not representing purely American interests. He is representing the interests of freedom, of religion, and of civilization. So is the pope. So are the other actors in Europe who joined them, like Helmut Kohl and Margaret Thatcher and others."[21]

Still, the pope and the president did not neglect the practical steps needed to translate their lofty mission into real-world strategy. O'Sullivan notes that the two leaders "sometimes coordinat[ed] their intelligence, sometimes coordinat[ed] their actions using each other's networks," all with the aim of bringing about "the spread of liberty and religious liberty to Central and Eastern Europe and to the Soviet Union."

Most important, they arranged to help Poland's Solidarity movement, especially after the Communists imposed martial law in December 1981. From 1982 through the June 1989 free elections in Poland, the United States funneled approximately $50 million to Solidarity.[22] Robert Gates, a top aide to CIA director Bill Casey who would later become secretary of defense, wrote in his memoirs: "We were most active in Poland. We slowly increased our clandestine support of Solidarity, mainly by providing printing equipment and other means of communication to the underground. They were not told that CIA was the source of the assistance, although there must have been suspicions.... We provided a good deal of money and equipment for the Polish underground for this."[23]

Where did the money go? It paid for "practical things," Craig Shirley says. "The money went for handbills.... It went to fund articles and speeches and ideas and support counter-protests.... It went for organization. It went for phones. It went for meetings." Later it went for a revolutionary new technology: the fax machine. Shirley explains the simple power of the fax in the mid-1980s: "They were using fax machines to send along articles and speeches and ideas and counter-protests and memos and things like that." That kind of technology was unheard of in Poland until clandestine funding brought it in.

Money was important, "but ultimately," Shirley concludes, "it was the power of ideas that spelled doom for the Soviet Union."

Whose ideas? Shirley later spoke to a group of Polish journalists and asked what had motivated them. "And to a person," Shirley says, "they said the words of Ronald Reagan and the words of John Paul II."

BRINGING FREEDOM

As this drama unfolded, the leader of the Solidarity movement, Lech Wałęsa, took on a prominent role. This charismatic electrician who worked in the Lenin Shipyard at Gdańsk gained strength and influence as his union fomented a series of strikes.[24] Strikes were illegal in Soviet satellite countries, but Solidarity kept growing. By 1981, Solidarity had some ten million members—nearly a third of Poland's population.[25]

The Communist rulers in Warsaw and Moscow panicked. In March, the Kremlin summoned Poland's general secretary, Stanisław Kania, and the new prime minister, General Wojciech Jaruzelski. Soviet despot Leonid Brezhnev tore into the Polish leaders for failing to control either the Solidarity movement or the Catholic Church.[26] As pressure mounted, Jaruzelski and Kania signed "The Central Concept of Introducing Martial Law in the Territory of the Polish People's Republic," a document that established a "legal" rationale for a full-scale Soviet Bloc invasion to "liquidate Solidarity."[27]

That invasion never came to pass.[28] But on December 13, the Polish government—helpless to corral Solidarity—imposed martial law. The Communists arrested Wałęsa and rounded up thousands of other union leaders, dissidents, and intellectuals. They persecuted clergy as well.

Faith and freedom fell under attack. Neither Reagan nor John Paul II could stand for that.

In imposing martial law, the Communists forgot one fact, Craig Shirley says: "For every action there is an equal and opposite reaction. The harder the Soviets crack down on Poland, the more Solidarity grows, the more important Lech Wałęsa becomes, the more important the need for freedom."

Reagan responded, but he did so prudently, playing the long game.

"He understood that he couldn't get everything he wanted," H. W. Brands notes. "He was a pragmatist as well as a visionary. And he understood that progress comes in steps. So when he took measured sanctions against the Soviet Union in response to the imposition of martial law in Poland, it wasn't as though he was retreating from his beliefs. This one step, even if primarily symbolic, told the world and told the Polish people *we are on your side*."

Poles knew they could look not only to themselves but also to Reagan and America, as well as to their Church and their native son in the Vatican. Other Western powers sided with them as well.

"There is strength in numbers," Shirley adds, "and by combining the power of London and Washington and Rome, they created a formidable front to the Soviet Union, and they could chip away at Soviet power, starting with Poland."

And chip away they did. Over time, the pope and the president widened their focus beyond aid Solidarity in Poland. They had a larger goal in mind: to take down an Evil Empire.

ACT IV

9

CODE NAME: CAPPUCCINO

Whatever the schemes of a heavenly plan, an earthly plan unfolded after the pope and the president met at the Vatican in June 1982. That earthly plan has not received the attention it deserves, largely because the Reagan White House and John Paul II's Vatican kept the partnership discreet. For the players involved, flexibility became essential. Improvising many of their lines, they performed their roles with vigor, verve—*con brio*.

The driving forces behind this plan were, on the American side, Bill Clark at the National Security Council (NSC) and Bill Casey at the CIA and, on the Vatican side, Archbishop Pio Laghi, the apostolic nuncio in Washington. They worked together to serve President Reagan and Pope John Paul II, and to advance the Divine Plan.

"A SOURCE OF GREAT JOY TO ME"

Washington and the Vatican began interacting in 1981, courtesy of Dick Allen and others.

Allen emphasizes an important reason that the Reagan White House began collaborating with the Vatican so early and so effectively: many of Reagan's top advisers on foreign policy, national security, and intelligence were Catholic, including Allen, Clark, and Casey. Allen points out that "it was the Reagan administration that gave full diplomatic status to the Vatican." The Reagan administration extended formal diplomatic recognition to the Holy See in early 1984; previously "there had just been a papal representative in Washington," as Allen says.

Yet it would be a mistake to see Reagan's Catholic advisers as pulling the strings without Reagan's knowledge. As Carl Bernstein reported in his 1992 *Time* cover story, "The mission would have been impossible without the full support of Reagan, who believed fervently in both the benefits and the practical applications of Washington's relationship with the Vatican."[1]

From the beginning, Archbishop Laghi served as a crucial conduit between the Vatican and the White House. Allen recalls his first meeting with Laghi, which began a close partnership between the Reagan administration and John Paul II's Vatican. The meeting occurred in 1981, during the new Reagan White House's first diplomatic reception.

The ambassadors of various foreign countries lined up according to precedence, meaning that the longest-serving representative stood first in line to greet the president while the newest appointee remained at the end of the line. Laghi had just been appointed.

Allen remembers how the stars aligned that evening:

> I was at the very end of the line with my wife, Pat.... And the person right in front of us was Archbishop Pio Laghi, who had flown up the day before from Argentina, where he had been ambassador. And now he was going to be [papal] representative to the United States.... And so we stood in line. And you can imagine when the 116 ambassadors and their wives going through a line to meet the president that I had about forty-five minutes or fifty minutes with Archbishop Pio Laghi. And I knew immediately that we had a ten-strike in this man. He had the full confidence of the pope. I could tell that he wasn't bluffing. He was earnest, down to earth,

and that was a source of great joy to me that I discussed with the president later on. And I was able to then work with Pio Laghi from time to time in an important way to get messages through to the Vatican.

Asked about the nature of those messages, Allen states (perhaps with understatement), "From time to time we needed to get a message through to the Vatican, and not necessarily to the pope, but for some other reason dealing with Eastern Europe or imprisonment or human rights or whatever it might be, and I very happily used later Cardinal, [then] Archbishop Pio Laghi."

Allen helped set the foundation for the relationship. He adds that his successor at the NSC, Bill Clark, continued the dialogue "very effectively."

Indeed, Clark stepped up the process when he took the helm at the NSC in 1982. He wanted the president to have the best information possible about his lead objectives.

A DISCREET WORKING GROUP

Bill Clark and Bill Casey came up with a code name for their working group with Pio Laghi: *cappuccino.*

The designation derived from the fine Italian coffee that Archbishop Laghi always prepared for Clark and Casey. Genuine Italian cappuccino was a rare commodity in Washington in the early 1980s, and the two Americans loved it.[2]

Clark and Casey spoke constantly, usually by telephone, as a means of "checking in" on the latest developments in this hot time of the Cold War. This might mean Nicaragua, Cuba, El Salvador, Afghanistan, the USSR, Poland, Rome. Depending on the subject, they often checked in with Pio Laghi as well. Always alert to the possibility that their phone lines might be bugged, Clark would signal to Casey their need to consult Laghi by saying simply, "Would you like to have some cappuccino?"

This meant a ride over to Laghi's residence on Connecticut Avenue in Washington, where the three would exchange news and views on the latest happenings of concern to Washington and Rome, especially actions related to Poland. Clark and Casey shared intelligence with Laghi and briefed him on the administration's position, and Laghi returned the favor by sharing the Vatican's knowledge. Clark and Casey would then report back to President Reagan, while Laghi communicated with the pope.

Sometimes the discussions signaled a need for Laghi to come to the White House and meet with Reagan directly. The archbishop went to the White House for meetings on at least six occasions, each time entering through the southwest gate to avoid the press.[3] Sometimes after the conversations at Laghi's residence, Clark or Casey (usually Casey) would fly to the Vatican to meet with John Paul II.

Clark stressed that his and Casey's conversations with Pio Laghi always occurred "back channel." The discussions were so sensitive that no note takers were permitted. They became a regular occurrence. According to Clark, he, Casey, and Laghi "would meet, in one or another way." Clark had the highest respect for Laghi, whom he called "a wonderful man."[4] Even his wife, Joan, came to know the future cardinal.

The three men who served John Paul II and Reagan in these private meetings also believed in a Divine Plan.

Two of those men seemed natural fits for the role. Laghi, of course, was an archbishop in the Roman Catholic Church. Bill Clark had entered seminary and remained a devout Catholic throughout his life. Together with Reagan, he coined the acronym "The DP."

But what about Bill Casey?

Did Reagan's wild CIA director really think of himself as acting according to God's will?

Yes, he did.

Herb Meyer, Casey's right-hand man at the CIA, saw a man on a mission.

Meyer notes that Casey, the former Wall Street lawyer and Nixon administration official, "was drifting into an affluent retirement when Ronald Reagan called." Reagan tapped Casey to run his 1980 presidential campaign, and then "the next thing you knew, he was CIA director," Meyer says. This turn of events made a huge impression on the "very patriotic" and "deeply religious" Casey.

"When he wound up running the CIA, Bill thought God had given him one more shot," Meyer says. "He wasn't going to waste it."[5]

One more shot to do what? Meyer states unequivocally: "To take out the Soviet Union."

Bill Casey, another devout Catholic, wanted to play his part in the DP. And so he, Casey, and Laghi took on vital roles in the Cold War drama.

ONE-ON-ONE WITH THE POPE

Casey's and Clark's cappuccino partner, Pio Laghi, became an unsung hero in the joint Washington-Vatican effort.

In the early 1980s, a young priest named Timothy Dolan worked at the papal nunciature in Washington. Dolan, now archbishop of New York, insists he was not privy to strategic information or anything on the "military side of things," but he certainly saw that "there were mutual allies on both sides, and friends of Reagan that became friends of John Paul II and who became much more welcome at the Holy See and vice versa." And those relationships "really made this providential friendship and sharing a vision much more possible." Dolan gives "a lot of credit to the Reagan administration for being uncharacteristic in its appreciation for the role of religion in the world."

A key Reagan administration figure to show such appreciation, in addition to Allen, Casey, and Clark, was General Vernon Walters. The lifelong diplomat and intelligence official has gone largely unrecognized for his efforts, when in fact he became "the principal emissary between Washington and Rome," as Bernstein reported. Citing Vatican sources, Bernstein wrote that Walters met with the pope "perhaps a dozen times," and "it wasn't supposed to be known that Walters was there."[6]

That estimate is probably about right. In his memoir, Walters related that he visited the Vatican two or three times a year over the course of about four years. Walters, who spoke at least seven languages, conducted these visits as President Reagan's uniquely delegated "ambassador-at-large."

Walters, a devout Catholic, said that his visits with John Paul II carried special meaning. "No assignment was more welcome in my public career than that given to me during the Reagan administration to brief this man I had respected and admired for many years," Walters wrote. His initial assignment came in 1981, when Bill Clark served as deputy secretary of state under Alexander Haig. Clark and Haig instructed Walters to meet with John Paul II at "regular intervals and explain to him U.S. policies in the fields of foreign affairs and defense." Walters noted "a convergence of interests between the Catholic Church and the United States in seeking to contain Communist expansion." Reagan knew it, Clark knew it, and Haig knew it. "According to my instructions, I was to present the facts based on the best intelligence available."[7]

Walters met one-on-one with John Paul II, with each session lasting about forty minutes. "He always received me alone," Walters recounted, "and whenever anyone attempted to interrupt the briefing, he would wave him out of the room."[8] The American ambassador discussed missile threats, conventional forces, the status of the Soviet air force and navy, problems in Poland, and even, on one occasion, what Walters described as "developments in the concentration camps in the Soviet Union that were then still operating." The pontiff's questions, Walters said, "were generally penetrating and insightful," and "at the end of each briefing he always thanked me for coming to 'enlighten his ignorance.'" Sometimes the pope would tell the ambassador "what subjects he would like next time."

Bernstein described a typical meeting between Walters and John Paul II: Walters placed an envelope on the table for the pontiff. In it were satellite photographs.

The pope immediately recognized a photo of the Lenin Shipyard in Gdańsk, where Solidarity was born. Then he pointed to a dark circle visible in the photo and asked, "What is this?" The answer: heavy equipment—tanks and other military vehicles for Polish security forces.[9]

They looked at other satellite images showing missiles programmed to reach Western Europe in minutes. They also studied photos of Polish troops that Walters said were ready to fight back if Warsaw Pact troops invaded.

To Walters, the importance of these meetings lay not in the information he supplied as much as in the information he *received* from John Paul II. The pope knew a lot about the internal situation in Poland. Walters, like Reagan, believed that the pope represented the real power in Poland, even as he sat in the Vatican (which John Paul II called "the golden cage"). The pope also had what Walters called "the oldest intelligence service in the world."

Cardinal Dolan expands on this idea: "[John Paul II] knew that the Holy See, which is the official word for the pope's universal jurisdiction over the Church, was an enormously helpful listening post in the whole world, probably the best one. And Reagan was shrewd enough to use that."

Similarly, Frank Shakespeare, Reagan's second ambassador to the Vatican, contended that "the Vatican is unrivaled as a listening post."[10]

Bernstein backs these assertions: "On military questions, American intelligence was better than the Vatican's, but the Church excelled in its evaluations of the political situation and in understanding the mood of the people."[11]

John Paul II biographer George Weigel affirms that the pope did not need a lot of intelligence gathered by the United States because he had an "intelligence network of his own" in Poland. Nonetheless, "he was grateful for what the American intelligence community could share with him because that would help him form his own prudential judgments about what was to be done."

BILL CASEY'S WINDOWLESS BLACK PLANE

Often as an outgrowth of his "cappuccino" diplomacy with Pio Laghi, Bill Casey secretly traveled to the Vatican for classified intelligence briefings.

Casey's son-in-law, Owen Smith, says that Casey and Walters flew to the Vatican so frequently that it seemed as if "they took turns going over there." "They made a lot more visits there than records indicate," Smith says, "and very often met with the Holy Father privately." According to Smith, Casey took no notes, just as he and Clark took no notes during their Laghi meetings.[12]

The CIA director flew to Rome "with the president's blessing," Dick Allen observes, and he kept his Vatican meetings secret by flying in what Allen calls "his specially equipped windowless C-141 jet, painted black."[13]

Though Allen ran the NSC only in the first year of the Reagan presidency, he retains knowledge of what happened in the years immediately thereafter. He speaks to Casey's role in particular but also to the input of others mentioned here.

"Let us not forget," Allen says, "that William J. Casey, the director of the Central Intelligence Agency, a great friend of mine of many, many years before and after the Reagan presidency, was from time to time getting in his black airplane and flying to Rome, landing and being taken directly to the Holy Father." Allen recounts that Casey provided the pope with classified intelligence briefings on Soviet movements in and around Poland, on Soviet missile placements, and similar matters. He gives an example: "I shared some overhead photos, some satellite photos with Bill Casey, and I know that he took some of those to Rome to show to the Holy Father." Allen notes that Casey "wouldn't actually brief the Holy Father about what our strategies might be," but he would "put a satellite photograph down on the ground and [see] if the pope had certain questions—*what is this* or *what is that?*" The photos might show, for example, Soviet mobile missiles placed in Eastern Europe, in "violation of a treaty specifying that nuclear weapons would be east of the Ural Mountains." Such evidence of Soviet treachery "was something that was of very great interest to the Holy Father."

Allen notes the important roles of Bill Clark, Vernon Walters, and (less so, but not to be neglected) Secretary of Defense Caspar Weinberger. He says that the Reagan plan with the Vatican "was indeed pushed forward in a very important way by Bill Casey and by Vernon Walters."

Marek Jan Chodakiewicz recounts an episode he heard about from Casey's son-in-law Owen Smith. Smith chairs the board of the Institute of World Politics, where Chodakiewicz serves as history professor. Smith told Chodakiewicz of one incident in which Casey—independently wealthy from his years on Wall Street—deposited $90,000 from his personal bank account into an account in London to buy printing presses. He asked Smith to help him arrange to have the printing presses directed to the Vatican "because the Holy Father will know exactly what to do with them" in Poland. "This was a private initiative," Chodakiewicz emphasizes. "The director of the CIA realized that his institution [the CIA] was not fit to react to meet the challenge immediately. It's a bureaucracy, so Casey himself helped. The CIA, as an institution, took its sweet time."

Such "private initiatives" were not uncommon. Former CIA director Robert Gates publicly recounted how Casey once sent $18,000 in cash for Solidarity to former Carter national security adviser Zbigniew Brzezinski. As Gates recalled the incident, Brzezinski complained to Casey at a Washington party that funding for one of his "favorite Polish covert actions" had been reduced. When Casey asked how much it would take to remedy the problem, Brzezinski estimated about $18,000. According to Gates: "The next day, a man showed up in Brzezinski's office, unannounced and unidentified, and handed Zbig a briefcase containing $18,000 in cash. Brzezinski, more than a little nonplussed, nevertheless passed it to a Polish visitor on his way home—where Lech Wałęsa and his compatriots put it to good use."[14]

Even Anne Applebaum, a journalist and historian who was by no means a CIA operative, notes that as a student in the late 1980s she took money to Solidarity activists. "It was a very common thing to do," she says. Western visitors naturally sympathetic to the Solidarity cause would bring in money, sometimes from their own pockets and other times from foundations and other sources. "You would bring it to people to help them print papers or print books or conduct opposition activity," Applebaum says.

THE INTELLIGENCE EXCHANGE

So we know that the partnership between Ronald Reagan and John Paul II extended so far as to include the exchange of classified intelligence. What are we to make of this exchange?

"I'm sure people find it fascinating that the pope was meeting with U.S. intelligence operatives," George Weigel says. "That is not a completely unique situation with John Paul II." Keep in mind Weigel's comment, supported by other accounts, that the pope had an extensive "intelligence network of his own."

Meanwhile, Weigel suggests that Ronald Reagan's willingness to share information with John Paul II demonstrated his "confidence in the pope." Reagan "ordered CIA director Casey to not only share the product, the intelligence product, with John Paul II, but to share the sources with him as well, including this very famous case of Colonel Ryszard Kukliński."

Kukliński, a high-ranking figure in the Polish Defense Ministry, became a mole for the Americans because he detested what Moscow had done to his homeland. Weigel rightly notes that Kukliński became "an invaluable source of information when it did look in December 1980 as if the Soviet army and allied War-

saw Pact armies were going to invade Poland to crush the nascent Solidarity movement." In a secret report he delivered to the United States, the Polish colonel outlined the Kremlin's plans to cross the border with eighteen divisions and to round up Solidarity leaders.[15] Later, in September 1981, Kukliński warned the United States that "the first steps have already been taken" toward martial law. The Polish Communist regime imposed martial law just three months later.[16]

In all, Kukliński passed tens of thousands of pages of secret Communist documents to the United States. The information he relayed proved vital to stopping the Kremlin.[17]

And just as Kukliński shared information with the United States, the United States shared information with its allies in the Vatican. Reagan, John Paul II, and their teams established a unique form of "cappuccino" diplomacy. And it soon took its toll on the seemingly mighty Soviet regime.

10

THE SOVIET HAND
AT WORK

The partnership that developed between the pope and the president would have been an impossibility had Soviet Communism had its way on May 13, 1981.

Ever since the attempt on John Paul II's life that day, questions
have swirled: Who did it? Who ordered the hit on the pope? Who
operated in concert with Mehmet Ali Agca?

It soon emerged that Agca's accomplices included Bulgarians.
But few people who knew about the devious ways of the Kremlin
believed that the Bulgarians had acted on their own in hiring an
assassin. From the very beginning, Ronald Reagan, Bill Casey, and
Bill Clark suspected a Soviet hand.

"The Bulgarian connection is what first raised flags," Clark
said. "It looked like Bulgaria was involved. And just about everything Bulgaria did was at the behest of the KGB." Besides, Clark
insisted, "The Bulgarians had no incentive or motive to do this on
their own. And it was the typical pattern of the Soviets to always
get someone else to do their dirty work."[1]

No Soviet Bloc regime did Moscow's dirty work quite like Bulgaria did. Bulgaria's leaders, military, intelligence apparatus, and
secret police proved such willing stooges of Moscow that people
joked that Bulgaria was effectively the sixteenth Soviet republic.

The Italian press raised doubts right away about Agca's acting alone, as did American journalist Claire Sterling, who did some of the best reporting on the attempted murder of the Vicar of Christ. Bill Casey was impressed by Sterling's level of detail and her ability to pick up discrepancies in Agca's accounts. In her front-page article in the June 10, 1984, edition of the *New York Times*, head-lined "Bulgaria Hired Agca to Kill Pope," she strongly suggested a Soviet hand at work.

The CIA's Herb Meyer arranged a private lunch between his boss and Sterling in New York, at Casey's request.

Certain members of the Reagan team knew the Soviets were capable of assassination; an Evil Empire does evil. Over time their suspicion turned into conviction. Eventually a supertight, super-secret internal CIA investigation concluded that the Soviets had ordered the hit on the pope.[2]

Casey commissioned that investigation, keeping it secret from the CIA "establishment." Many establishmentarians dismissed out of hand the possibility of Soviet involvement in the shooting; they could not conceive of such Soviet iniquity.

Facing this institutional opposition within his own agency, Casey authorized his own internal investigation into Moscow's role in what William Safire of the *New York Times* called the "crime of the century."

One of the few people who saw the highly classified report described it to Paul Kengor: "About thirty pages [in length]. Eyes only. Really, really tight. Only one or two copies.... This was so classified that they practically took the eyeballs out of the corpses.... I've *never, ever* seen *anything* that classified." The source joked, "The last thing I saw, we were burning out the eyes of the girl who typed it."

"I don't know where it is today," the source added. "That document has never come out. People don't know it, but that's what they really want. That has the answer." He affirmed, "The document that I'm referring to answers the question [on the shooting of the pope]."

The report provides a crystal-clear answer, the source said: "The Soviets did it. They shot the pope."

Even those who suspected that the Soviets orchestrated the hit missed the true culprits. Most pointed the finger at the KGB. But the CIA's secret investigation concluded that Soviet military intelligence, the dreaded GRU, planned the assassination attempt, albeit with the blessing of the head of the KGB, Yuri Andropov— who became Soviet general secretary in November 1982. An Italian commission that investigated the shooting and other researchers likewise concluded that the GRU organized the effort.

"THE PHYSICAL ELIMINATION OF JP II"

The Soviet leadership may have signaled its evil intentions early on. Decades after the fact, journalist and Cold War historian John Koehler discovered a shocking document dated November 13, 1979. On that date, the Soviet state's Secretariat of the Central Committee issued this chilling edict: "Use all possibilities available to the Soviet Union to prevent the new course of policies initiated by the Polish pope; if necessary with additional measures beyond disinformation and discreditation."[3]

Nine leaders at the top of the Soviet Communist hierarchy signed this edict, including the fast-rising Mikhail Gorbachev.

A number of sources have since read that document, beginning with Italy's military intelligence and security service, SISDE (Servizio per le Informazioni e la Sicurezza Democratica). The Italian government added this arresting note at the bottom of the Soviet order: "SISDE says document found in Moscow points to plan for the 'physical elimination of JP II.'"[4]

John Koehler agreed. The longtime Associated Press reporter, who covered the Soviet Bloc for years, wrote, "In layman's terms, this was an order for assassination."[5]

Not everyone shares that view, however. "I've read the memo," George Weigel says, "and I don't think there is any direct line between that memo and what happened on May 13, 1981, because no one would have written down, 'Go shoot the pope.' That is not the way the game worked.... These things simply did not work that way. No one would have been stupid enough to put in easily decodable language an order to eliminate the pope."[6]

Craig Shirley offers a different perspective. "Bureaucrats love to see their names in writing," he says. "Bureaucrats love to commit things to paper. And it doesn't matter whether it's a bureaucrat in the Kremlin or a bureaucrat in Washington." In his own extensive historical research, he has uncovered many government documents "that deal with unpleasant outcomes or unpleasant activities." For example: "I've found many documents on World War II that ended up being very embarrassing to the Franklin Roosevelt administration, but they were still there. They were still in writing."

Mikhail Gorbachev has denied that the Central Committee document constituted an order to kill John Paul II. In a January 2000 interview with the Italian newspaper *Il Tempo*, Gorbachev said the document plainly intended to "discredit the actions of the pope" and referred to "political actions," "political measures," and "propaganda," with no "ulterior actions" aimed at John Paul II's physical health. "Nothing was ordered against the pope as a person, and it could not be otherwise," the former Soviet leader concluded. "At that time, similar action had been eliminated and forbidden from the KGB's arsenal."[7]

The language of the order does leave room for interpretation. Still, Gorbachev's disavowals remain questionable. For example, despite his claim that the document merely sought to "discredit the actions of the pope" with standard "propaganda" measures, the document called for "*additional measures beyond* disinformation and discreditation [emphasis added]." The Central Committee ordered the use of "all possibilities" to stop the pope—a frightening prospect from a regime responsible for the deaths of tens of millions of its own citizens.

Nor did this order represent the only evidence that the Soviets were considering physical violence against the pope. As Koehler reported, a KGB defector disclosed that when he visited Poland in 1979, KGB head Yuri Andropov sent a cable demanding information on how to "get physically close" to the pope.[8] The KGB officer, Major Victor Sheymov, told American reporters after he defected: "In the KGB slang, it was clearly understood that when you say physically close, there was only one reason to get close: to assassinate him. Words like *murder* or *assassinations* are never used. They have substituted gentler terms."[9]

Gorbachev himself may not have meant to call for the killing of the pope when he signed the document. And he very well may not have had any personal knowledge of the plot against the pope that ensued, since only a tiny number of Soviet officials would have been involved. Gorbachev did not become general secretary until March 1985.

Although Weigel does not see that November 1979 Soviet document as a "smoking gun," he acknowledges, "What the memorandum does confirm is the gravity of the threat that [Moscow] perceived." Moreover, he cannot dismiss the idea that the Soviets were complicit in the shooting of John Paul II on May 13, 1981. "I am quite convinced," he says, "that whatever causal chain leads us to 1981 finally ends in Moscow and probably at Lubyanka [KGB headquarters]." Weigel adds that "no one who thinks carefully about the question who would benefit by the assassination of John Paul II, which is the crucial question, doubts that" the Soviets set the plot in motion.

When asked to comment on Moscow's role in the attempt on the pope's life, John O'Sullivan says: "Was the Soviet Union behind it? Well, put it like this, there is no way that the Bulgarian secret service is going to attempt to murder this pope, any pope, without clearing it with the Soviet Union. It is just inconceivable." Sullivan states: "We know who shot the pope. It's a young Turkish extremist working at this point for the Bulgarian secret service."

O'Sullivan notes that the Soviets used the Bulgarian secret service to carry out murders in the West from time to time. He cites the case of Georgi Markov, a Bulgarian defector living in

London and working as a journalist for the BBC World Service. Markov had run afoul of Communist censors before he defected, and his radio broadcasts critiquing Communist regimes made him even more of an enemy of Bulgaria and the Kremlin. In September 1978, a Communist agent poisoned the dissident journalist on London's Waterloo Bridge. The agent used an umbrella to fire a poison dart containing ricin at Markov. He took out his target: Markov died, despite the best efforts of doctors to save him.

"That was a very revealing scandal," notes O'Sullivan. "And in this case, they were behind the operation."

By "they," he means the Communists of Bulgaria and the USSR, working in tandem.

The Markov murder suggests another reason to doubt Mikhail Gorbachev's denials about the November 1979 Central Committee order. The Communists killed Markov only a year before that order came down, offering powerful evidence that assassinations had not in fact "been eliminated and forbidden from the KGB's arsenal."

THE SOVIETS DID IT

In 2006 a special commission of the Italian parliament concluded an exhaustive investigation into the shooting of John Paul II. The investigation concluded—"beyond any reasonable doubt"—that "the leadership of the Soviet Union took the initiative to eliminate Pope John Paul II." The order came directly from Soviet general secretary Leonid Brezhnev, who gave the job to the supersecret GRU. The report also confirmed the Bulgarian connection, though the commission reported that the Bulgarian role served mainly to divert attention and responsibility from the Soviet Union.[10]

Despite this report—and the diligent work of other researchers and reporters since the 1980s, plus the CIA's own secret findings—some observers maintain that we don't have a clear paper trail to prove Moscow's role in the assassination attempt.

To that, O'Sullivan responds: "We don't expect to find paper trails. This would have been something that would have been maintained at a very, very small, secret, high level." He adds: "I think there is little doubt that [the Soviets] did in fact order his death, even though we are not able to trace completely everything that happened. We can draw a reasonable historical conclusion." O'Sullivan expands on this point:

> From the moment that John Paul II became the pope, there was acute nervousness and discussion in Moscow about how to handle him. It was recognized that he was a threat, but a threat that they didn't altogether know what to do with.... So, yes, there was an attempt to murder the most serious threat to the Soviet Union in the form of any human being who had emerged since 1917. And it was made very difficult for them because a pope is someone whom the world recognizes. This is somebody who is something more important than the most distinguished politician. This particular pope was in fact raising great moral issues from a high level. And finally, he himself had said he was a threat...it was almost one of the first things he had said after becoming pope. He said about the Church of Eastern Europe, "The Church of Eastern Europe is no longer the Church of silence because it speaks with my voice." I think the Soviets drew the same conclusion and they decided that by hook or by crook he had to go, and that's what then happened.

Asked whether the Soviets played a role in the assassination attempt, Craig Shirley says bluntly, "Of course they did." He points to the mounting pressures on Moscow as motivation: "The Soviets were under siege every day throughout the 1980s. There are new threats to them. There is the Solidarity movement. There is the Velvet Revolution in Czechoslovakia. There is democratic revolution going on in Hungary. They are under siege. They are paranoid. They are going to do everything they can to defend [and] hold on to what they already have. Of course, it makes perfect sense that they knew of or had a hand in the attempted assassination of John Paul II."

Like O'Sullivan, Shirley points to the danger that the Polish pope posed: "As Pope John Paul II becomes more popular as his power grows, as his influence extends, he is a moral threat to the very existence of the Soviet Union. And they can't allow him to continue. So, at least, there is a conspiracy of thinking that they had to deal with him and maybe deal with him brutally."

Anne Applebaum speaks just as emphatically about Soviet culpability. "Of course they tried to assassinate him," she says. "They understood exactly how dangerous he was as an ideological force." An expert on the Soviet Bloc, Applebaum emphasizes how closely tied the Bulgarians were to Moscow: "They wouldn't have done it on their own. The fact that the Soviet Union tried to assassinate John Paul II through the mechanism of a Bulgarian assassin tells you exactly how frightened of him they were." To those who say that Mehmet Ali Agca acted alone or that the Bulgarian government acted without Moscow's knowledge, she replies, "I find that very hard to believe." She explains: "In that period and at that time, the secret services of all of those countries were very much under the KGB's roof, and it would have been a KGB decision to use the Bulgarians to carry something like that out."

Such were the suspicions of the core group around the pope and around Ronald Reagan after the shooting.

Bill Clark gave an indication of those suspicions in a rare public statement he made in Las Vegas on August 18, 1984, at a reunion of army counterintelligence veterans.

It was an intimate, fairly small gathering, but a public event nonetheless. No press bothered to show, meaning that reporters missed a striking line that Clark personally penciled into the speech. The typed speech featured this line: "It wouldn't be at all surprising if a similar [disinformation] campaign was now under way to discredit the Italian investigation into the attempted murder of Pope John Paul II." (In fact, just such a campaign was well under way.) Clark replaced the period at the end of the sentence with a comma and then wrote in these previously unspoken words: "which suggests a Bulgarian and therefore Soviet connection."[11]

"THANK YOU, BUT NOT NOW"

John Paul II harbored his own suspicions about the Soviets, but he did not want details of the Kremlin conspiracy exposed.

The pope reportedly knew the results of Bill Casey's closely held CIA investigation. According to Owen Smith, who served on the CIA director's security detail at the time, Casey used one of his secret trips to the Vatican to brief the Holy Father on the CIA team's finding that the Soviets had planned the shooting. Smith says that Casey's information did not surprise John Paul II.

But Casey's son-in-law provides another crucial detail: he says that the pope asked the Reagan administration to keep quiet about its information on the Soviets' role in the shooting.

Consider the context: The 1980s had intensified fears of World War III between two nuclear-armed superpowers. Imagine if the news came out that the U.S. government had discovered a Soviet-orchestrated assassination attempt on the leader of the world's largest religion, who provided a voice for those suffering under Soviet Communism.

The pope recognized an opportunity as well. Casey's team finalized its report in the spring of 1985, just as a new and decidedly different Soviet leader took power: Mikhail Gorbachev. With Gorbachev now leading the Soviet Union, the Vatican could open dialogue with Moscow. The pope did not want to jeopardize that opportunity.[12]

By 1989, the Vatican's dialogue with Moscow had advanced quite a bit, so much so that John Paul II and Gorbachev would have their first meeting at the end of the year. Thomas Melady, the ambassador to the Holy See under new president George H.W. Bush, sat down with John Paul II in October. Melady recounted the meeting after the pope's death in 2005. "In his very calm voice," Melady wrote, "Pope John Paul II told me that he did not want the United States government to make an issue of the 1981 plot to assassinate him." The new ambassador said that he wanted the U.S. government to dig deeper into the plot, but the pope responded, "No, not now."[13]

Melady died in 2014. His friend Marek Jan Chodakiewicz says that the former ambassador's private account of that first meeting with John Paul II differed from the one he published. According to Chodakiewicz, Melady did not tell the pope that he wanted the U.S. government to "continue the investigation" (as Melady wrote in 2005). Instead, he told the pontiff that "on orders of" President Bush he was to communicate the U.S. government's willingness to *reveal information and release documents* on the failed assassination.

Chodakiewicz spoke openly about his Melady conversation during his interview for this book:

> I will share a classified anecdote by a late friend of mine, Ambassador Tom Melady, who was a U.S. envoy to the Holy See for George Bush senior. When Tom presented his credentials to the pope, he told John Paul II, "I have a secret personal message from the president of the United States. As you know, under Ronald Reagan, we initiated an investigation into the plot to kill the pope, and now the former vice president [Bush], now president of the United States, has tasked me with telling you that we can reveal things about the culprits, and you know who the culprits are: the Soviets." And John Paul II said, "Thank you, but not now."

Why "not now"? Chodakiewicz seconds a point Melady made in his 2005 article: John Paul II was nurturing a dialogue with Gorbachev. The Polish-born Chodakiewicz says that the pope was "working on Gorbachev for the Soviets to reveal the secret of the Katyn Massacre," one of the most infamous war crimes in the history of the Polish people. So John Paul II passed on putting a spotlight on "his own martyrdom, or the attempted assassination, in favor of the Soviets' owning up to the massacre of twenty-eight thousand Polish officers and other intelligentsia in 1940."

George Weigel sums up: "I think John Paul II deep in his heart of hearts knew who was ultimately behind this, but he didn't see any point in making a big deal about that. I think he was probably right not to do so."

The full CIA investigative report "has never come out," as our source told of a document he characterizes as perhaps the most classified he ever encountered in his career intelligence. We sincerely hope that the U.S. intelligence community reveals everything it knows about May 13, 1981.

And we hope a former KGB lieutenant colonel named Vladimir Putin reveals what role Russia played in *the* crime of the twentieth century.

11

"IT IS GOD'S WILL"

I f there was a glimmer of hope amid all of Moscow's malevolence, it was that the Evil Empire was at long last on the
mend...which means it was on its way to the grave.

A new leader appeared on the Soviet stage in 1985: Mikhail
Gorbachev.

Leonid Brezhnev had ruled over the empire for eighteen years,
but after his death in November 1982, the Soviets cycled through
two general secretaries in just two and a half years. Both Yuri
Andropov and Konstantin Chernenko suffered ill health for most
of their short terms and died in office.

Gorbachev, two decades younger than his predecessors,
emerged as a different kind of leader for the USSR. He would even
use these words to Ronald Reagan: "I am convinced it is God's will
that we should cooperate."[1]

Not the typical sentiment of a Soviet despot.

Gorbachev tried to make the USSR a better place. In doing so,
he would, inadvertently, usher it out of existence. Together with
a pope and a president, he would help bring a peaceful end to the
Cold War.

John Paul II would describe Gorbachev to colleagues and
friends as a "providential man," an instrument of Providence.[2]

Years later he said so publicly. In 1992 he described his relationship with Gorbachev to reporters from the Italian newspaper *La Stampa*: "There was something instinctive between us, as if we had already known each other. And I know why that was: our meeting had been prepared by Providence."[3]

The pope's biographer, George Weigel, shrewdly observes that Gorbachev seems an instrument of a Providence that the Soviet leader probably never understood as opposed to a conscious agent of a higher design.[4] Still, John Paul II saw the general secretary as performing the will of Providence (consciously or not) in terminating his Communist regime's seventy-year-old assault on religion and other basic freedoms.

BELIEVING IN A HIGHER POWER

Gorbachev rose quickly through the ranks of the Politburo in the 1970s and into the 1980s. When he became general secretary, he showed a willingness to work with others, especially the pope and the president, and even to extend freedom to religious believers.

He stood apart from other Soviet leaders in that he did not hate religion. His mother, two grandmothers, and one of his grandfathers were committed Orthodox Christians. His only grandparent who was not a religious believer, his grandfather, nonetheless "considered it a personal obligation to respect believers," Gorbachev later said. His deaconess mother had him baptized covertly as a baby—an unusual distinction for the future leader of an officially atheist state. When they were alone in their cottage, she would pull an icon from the wall or mantel and bless him with it. His grandmothers read him the Bible.[5]

Gorbachev shared details of his Christian roots in a June 1988 meeting with Cardinal Agostino Casaroli, the Vatican secretary of state. Casaroli later shared the account with the pope.[6]

Both John Paul II and Ronald Reagan thought—hoped—that Gorbachev might be a closet Christian.

The U.S. president held his first summit with Gorbachev in November 1985. Afterward, a perplexed but impressed Reagan told his close aide Michael Deaver, "I don't know, but I honestly think he believes in a higher power."[7]

Similarly, when the pope revealed his belief that his meeting with Gorbachev was "prepared by Providence," he added, "[Gorbachev] does not profess to be a believer, but with me I recall he spoke of the great importance of prayer and of the inner side of man's life."[8]

Did the Divine Plan ring for a Slavic Christian, or at least someone sympathetic to faith, to fill the slot of the last Soviet dictator—the final cast member in the dramatic end of the Cold War? That would provide quite a twist in the plot.

Gorbachev's entrance led to another plot twist, this one involving Reagan. Many observers viewed Reagan as a hawk, a Cold Warrior, the anti-Communist who lit up the USSR as the "focus of evil in the modern world." So they grew puzzled when he appeared so enthusiastic to sit down with a Soviet leader and cut weapons arsenals.

In fact, Reagan had sought to reduce nuclear weapons all along. The old Screen Actors Guild president knew how to establish a strong negotiating position.[9]

Few at the time understood this nuclear-abolitionist side of President Reagan. His detractors on the political left accused him of being a warmonger.

Today, however, even liberal historians concede that cutting nuclear weapons had been Reagan's intention.[10] James Mann, one of Reagan's more liberal biographers, acknowledges that the president was "horrified by the possibility of nuclear war, even during his first term in the White House."[11]

So Reagan was eager to sit down with a Soviet leader like Mikhail Gorbachev. "Reagan was a fairly persuasive guy," H. W. Brands says, "and he found someone in Gorbachev who was, for his own reasons, ready to make a deal."

Those negotiations took place at four major summits: Geneva

in November 1985, Reykjavik in October 1986, Washington in December 1987, and Moscow in May–June 1988.

"When he goes to Geneva or Reykjavik, he's really willing to say, *Let's abolish nuclear weapons,*" Douglas Brinkley says. "No American president of the Cold War really believed that that was plausible, but Reagan is willing to say, *Look, anything to make the world a better and safer and ultimately more democratic place, then I'm willing to go that extra mile.*"

In that sense, Brinkley says, Reagan the supposed Cold War hawk became the unexpected "peace warrior." This development pleased John Paul II, who was especially concerned about the prospects of nuclear war.

Decades removed from these discussions, we can easily fail to grasp just how enormous the stakes were. The possibility of nuclear war posed a real and terrifying threat, one that hung over every exchange between the United States and the USSR.

Cold War historian Stephen Kotkin reminds us of those stakes: "The Soviet Union had the power to end the world many times over, so it really was an existential threat. It was the kind of threat that previous regimes, even the Nazi and the Japanese regime, didn't possess. For all the havoc, the death, and destruction that the Nazis and the Japanese exerted during World War II, the Soviet Union was in a different category."

For this reason, Kotkin titled his book on the last decades of the Soviet Union *Armageddon Averted.*[12]

The Kremlin had that doomsday capability. "And Reagan was willing to stand up to them despite the awesome capabilities that they had," Kotkin adds. "And he was willing to do so even when he was criticized. For example, for calling them an Evil Empire, for positioning additional nuclear weapons in Europe to show that we meant business and wouldn't back down. And this message got across in Moscow that Reagan was a serious person to be dealt with."

The message arguably helped lead to Mikhail Gorbachev as Soviet leader. Members of the Politburo deemed the young, energetic, and intelligent Gorbachev the one who could go toe-to-toe with Reagan.[13]

THE CONFLUENCE OF CHARACTERS

By the mid-1980s, we see three headliners on the world stage. But it is important to enter from the wings a fourth essential player.

"Margaret Thatcher, we can't leave her out," Cardinal Timothy Dolan reminds us. Nearly every authority interviewed for this book mentioned the British prime minister.

John O'Sullivan, who worked for Thatcher, certainly agrees: "Wojtyła, Thatcher, and Reagan all embodied such fading virtues as faith, self-reliance, and patriotism."[14] O'Sullivan devoted an entire book to the subject: *The President, the Pope, and the Prime Minister.*

Kotkin marvels at "this cast of characters": "You had a British prime minister, a woman, who was committed to denationalization of the economy, to opening up markets, to standing up to authoritarian regimes abroad. Reagan, president of the United States, the superpower. The pope, the first non-Italian pope since the early sixteenth century. And then, of course, Gorbachev, the reform-minded, liberalizing, unwitting destroyer of Communism as general secretary of the party."

Kotkin continues:

It would be hard, if you were writing a script, if you were sitting out there in Burbank around a table, having recently graduated with an MFA from Yale and you were quite imaginative and creative and you wanted to set the scene for the late '70s, early '80s, a dramatic moment in time, you would have been very hard-pressed to think up these four characters. And moreover, these four characters at the same time. That confluence was phenomenal.

"We Got Lucky"

Three of those characters stood on one side. The fourth, Gorbachev, served as the antagonist. But he was not a stereotypical villain; he brought a new complexity to the role that heightened the drama of the Cold War's final act.

"I think the selection of Mikhail Gorbachev as chief of the Soviet Communist Party is best understood generationally," George Weigel says. "Unlike his three predecessors, Konstantin Chernenko, Yuri Andropov, and Leonid Brezhnev, Gorbachev did not see his closest friends dragged down into the basement of Lubyanka Prison in Moscow and assassinated with a bullet in the back of the head. He didn't have that cold, almost reptilian look that the others had."

Weigel recounts a telling scene from the first meeting between Gorbachev and John Paul II. He remembers verbatim what Gorbachev said in introducing the pope to his wife, Raisa: "I have the honor to present the greatest moral authority on Earth, and he's a Slav like us." As Weigel notes, that statement was "really quite striking." For starters, "it recognized a kind of kindred culture between Russia and Poland which is not the normal Russian attitude toward Poles." Gorbachev was saying, in effect, "We have something in common in our ethnic and cultural background."[15] And to have the leader of the USSR salute the pope as "the greatest moral authority on earth" indicated a break from the Soviet past.

Douglas Brinkley observes that Gorbachev represented an important change in the Soviet Union because he "was willing to recognize what was heinous and wrong with not just Stalinism, but the KGB and Brezhnev." Remarking on the pope's assessment of the "providential man," Brinkley argues that Gorbachev's ascension signaled "that the moment was right for change in the world." He concludes, "Both the pope and Reagan outstretched their arms because he was truly the change agent of the moment."

Gorbachev's role in this turbulent historical drama was a complicated one. He inherited a country with a crippled economy. The

Communist credos that had held sway since the Revolution of 1917 had long since proved unworkable. He promised to usher in a new era heralded by the slogans *glasnost* and *perestroika*. *Glasnost* meant a new openness in civil liberties and freedoms; *perestroika* promised reform and restructuring.

O'Sullivan says that in calling for such sweeping changes, Gorbachev "set out to do something that was unachievable—namely, to save the Soviet Union from its own sclerosis."

To be clear, Mikhail Gorbachev never sought the peaceful dissolution of the Soviet Union as a way to end the Cold War. On the contrary, he sought to improve the USSR precisely so he could save it.

But he could not contain the reforms he unleashed. Gorbachev opened the floodgates to a freedom tide that ultimately washed away the very USSR he had tried to preserve. In O'Sullivan's words, "He set off a chain of events that destroyed the system he was trying to save."

Of all those interviewed for this book, Stephen Kotkin in particular stresses Gorbachev's importance. He notes that the general secretary of the Communist Party of the Soviet Union began "unwittingly to dismantle his own system." Gorbachev "opened up, loosened up, and, as a result, destroyed that system." To be sure, Kotkin credits Reagan for how he handled Gorbachev, goaded Gorbachev, and "gave Gorbachev a lot of running room." But it was Gorbachev who undid the Soviet system from within—who introduced competitive elections, established legal markets in parts of the Soviet Communist economy, relaxed censorship, allowed alternative opinions, and permitted people to practice their faith openly. And unlike a Stalin, he did not resort to violence on a mass scale to hold that system together.

"We got lucky with Gorbachev," Kotkin says, "just as we got lucky with Reagan."

Reagan had foreseen what would happen once the Communists began loosening the chains on their people, especially those that shackled religion.

James Rosebush recalls a private conversation he had with the president just before the first Reagan-Gorbachev summit, in November 1985:

> The president and I were sitting in front of the roaring fire at the villa loaned to us in Geneva, waiting for the Gorbachev motorcade to arrive. And I said, "Mr. President, what do you think will really bring down Soviet-style Communism and Eastern Bloc totalitarianism?" And he looked at me and without skipping a beat said, "Oh, Jim, that's only going to happen because of the people's desire to know God." Obviously, I kept that in my heart. I didn't disclose it at the time.... But Reagan saw this, he knew this. Here he's telling me that the only way that we're going to bring down these systems that keep people from knowing God is to replace the worship of the state with the worship of God.

SAVING A STATE FOUNDED ON LIES

By the late 1980s, it was obvious to anyone paying attention that the Soviet empire was imploding, with religious forces rising to the fore. Permitting the worship of God dealt a heavy blow to atheistic Communism.

Weigel says that John Paul II respected Gorbachev as "a man who was prepared to risk power for what he thought was right." But he is quick to point out that "what Gorbachev thought was right was a reformed Communism," which was not at all the goal that the pope and the president pursued.

Although Gorbachev seemed "far more intelligent" than all his predecessors, Weigel says, "curiously, he never seemed to have figured out until the whole thing fell apart in 1991 that you can't reform something that is fundamentally mistaken in its basic ideas."

Gorbachev would learn the hard way that there was no salvaging the unsalvageable.

"Ironically," Craig Shirley observes, "it was Western liberalism, classical liberalism, which Gorbachev instituted with *glasnost* and *perestroika*, which are basically Western liberal ideas, that were his undoing."

Like O'Sullivan and Weigel, Anne Applebaum makes a point of saying that "Gorbachev himself didn't intend the Soviet Union to collapse." Instead, "he intended to reform it, and in reforming it, he almost accidentally first lost its empire and then allowed the whole system to collapse."

Applebaum analyzes the situation this way: "What Gorbachev didn't understand about his own country is that once you began speaking honestly about the way things are, people immediately began to want to speak honestly about everything, including the past." For example: "What had really happened under Stalin? What was the Gulag? Why did all those people disappear into nowhere? What happened to the people who were murdered in the 1930s? What was the real history of the Second World War? Didn't Stalin have a pact with Hitler in 1939? Isn't that the precursor of the war and not just the invasion of the Germans in 1941?"

Gorbachev's new openness—his *glasnost*—allowed people in the Soviet Union to ask such piercing questions out in the open for the first time. As a result, Applebaum says, *glasnost* exposed what so many intuitively knew: "The state was founded on a series of lies—lies about itself, lies about the economy, lies about the world." It was built on an "elaborate" network of lies: "The system lied about what it was doing; it lied about how it controlled people; it lied about what its goals were. It was fundamentally dishonest from the very beginning." It was, to borrow the language of Czech dissident Václav Havel, "the Communist culture of the lie."[16]

They would know the truth, and the truth would set them free.

Once people began to speak openly, Applebaum adds, even the members of the Communist Party establishment found it impossible to sustain the system or even to want to stay in power: "It's really an extraordinary moment when the whole ruling class in that whole region really just give up. They say: 'We don't really believe in this thing we're supporting anymore. We're not going to work for it anymore.'"

Applebaum invokes a stirring image from 1989 as a metaphor: "The guy who lifts the barrier to open the Berlin Wall is a security guard who sees all these people demonstrating in the streets. He's lived through this system all his life and suddenly he says: 'Why do I need to do this? This is ridiculous. There's *glasnost*, we can say what we want. I'm just opening it.' And he lets people through. That, I think, is a real metaphor for what happened. The system gave up once people were speaking honestly about how it had worked."

Gorbachev had once defended the Berlin Wall, but now he did not stop the free flow of humanity over that wall.[17] Here again, he helped unleash forces he did not anticipate and could not contain. The wall was only a temporary prop for a regime that could no longer hold its people captive. Those forces would overwhelm the Communist Bloc in Eastern Europe and Gorbachev's own position as head of an increasingly unstable Soviet Union.

Douglas Brinkley offers a similar appraisal: "I think Gorbachev didn't realize that once you let the genie out, that once you had freedom of religion, that it was going to be hard to suppress it again, that it became such a widespread movement in Russia, that they didn't know how to control or contain it."

Both Applebaum and Brinkley point out that Gorbachev's legacy in the West differs from that in his home country. Applebaum says, "Gorbachev, who is remembered as a great hero in the West, in Russia is remembered as the man who brought down the Soviet empire and as the man who triggered a decade's worth of economic hardship."

Gorbachev is "a conflicted historical figure," Brinkley comments: "Here in the United States we treat Gorbachev like a Nobel Prize–type of incredible world leader, where in his own country he is without honor and glory."

He remains a complicated character to assess.

THE FREEDOM GENIE

Ronald Reagan understood the forces that overwhelmed Mikhail Gorbachev. He understood them better than Gorbachev did, because Reagan, as an anti-Communist from the beginning, better understood human nature and human freedom. Ditto for Pope John Paul II.

"As is always the case," Reagan said in late 1990, "once people who have been deprived of basic freedom taste a little of it, they want all of it. It was as if Gorbachev had uncorked a magic bottle and a genie floated out, never to be put back in again."[18]

Craig Shirley elaborates on why Gorbachev could not put the freedom genie back in the bottle: "It is impossible to grant limited amounts of freedom. Because you give people a taste for freedom and they want more." Gorbachev was "actually unintentionally hollowing out the Soviet Union" by admitting that everything the system had stood for across seven decades had been wrong: "Collectivism didn't work, oppression didn't work, and we need new openness. We need new approaches to maybe a limited free-market economy and more political debate in this country. And it leads to his downfall, which leads to the temporary rise for a time of [Boris] Yeltsin, which leads ultimately to the dissolution of the Soviet Union."

Weigel reaches for a different metaphor: "Once a totalitarian state begins to acknowledge an elementary human right, it's like tugging on a thread on a tapestry. If you tug hard enough on that one thread, the whole thing is going to unravel. And that's what Gorbachev's policy of *glasnost* eventually did." In particular, when Gorbachev allowed for religious freedom, the tapestry unwound quickly—just as Ronald Reagan had predicted. "Religious freedom fundamentally means the state does not own my soul," Weigel says. "And if the state does not own my soul, it doesn't own what is most unique and distinctive to me. And [when] you get enough people understanding that and living that, you have a resistance movement that even the most brutal totalitarian power can't crush."

When it comes to the "chain of cause and effect," O'Sullivan believes that the real "man of Providence," so to speak, "was in fact Ronald Reagan in the sense of creating a challenge that the Soviet Union could not meet effectively." O'Sullivan would say the same, he adds, about John Paul II and Margaret Thatcher.

These were the key players on the world's stage in the thrilling closing act of the Cold War.

ACT V

12

"I DIDN'T BRING THE WALL DOWN"

Communism came crashing down in Eastern Europe in 1989. The world remembers the tumbling of the Berlin Wall in November as symbolizing the collapse. But the first rip in the Iron Curtain had come five months earlier, in June, when Poland held free and fair elections. The Communists did not win a single seat.

Just as Ronald Reagan and John Paul II had long figured, Poland served as the linchpin.

One year later, Lech Wałęsa was elected president of a free Poland. One year after that, Mikhail Gorbachev resigned his post as the last leader of the Soviet Union. The USSR officially dissolved, less than fifteen years after Reagan summed up his policy toward the Soviets as "We win and they lose." The Cold War was over.

Reagan refused to take personal credit for this epic achievement. He thanked God and the Divine Plan. Both Bill Clark and Dick Allen, Reagan national security advisers, remarked on Reagan's sense of the hand of Providence rather than his own.

"He did feel a calling, as I did, to this effort and the idea that truth would ultimately prevail," Clark said. "Not that *he* would prevail, but the truth would prevail." Clark recounted a scene he witnessed after the Communist implosion: "I remember one day I was with him when someone congratulated him for taking down the wall. He said, 'No, I didn't bring the wall down. That was part of the Divine Plan, teamwork, and God's will.' ... He just had total confidence in the divine will."[1] Clark cited Reagan's "number-one maxim": "We can accomplish anything if we don't concern ourselves with who gets the credit." The president lived that out, according to Clark: "This is an amazingly humble person. True humility. There was no pride there at all."[2]

Clark affirmed that view in other interviews and public testimonies on Reagan and the Cold War.

Allen agrees with Clark's assessment of Reagan's humility, saying that Reagan "would look back and say something like: 'Our team has fulfilled God's purpose.... We were part of the Divine Plan.'"[3]

Reagan said something similar in a speech a year after the USSR landed on the ash heap of history, just as he had predicted in 1982. Speaking in Oxford on December 4, 1992, the former president quoted from Winston Churchill's famous "Never Give In" address: "We must all thank God that we have been allowed, each of us according to our stations, to play a part in making these days memorable in the history of our race."[4]

The actor-turned-president had played a part, but he emphasized that we *all* can play a part.

John Paul II likewise did not want to take credit.

"I didn't cause this to happen," the pope later said of the Soviet meltdown. "The tree was already rotten. I just gave it a good shake and the rotten apples fell."[5]

The pope and the president wanted to give the credit to God and to many other forces, all within the divine scheme.

THE TIDE OF FREEDOM

The many sources interviewed for this book offered their perspectives on the concluding act of this drama. All lived through and watched what played out on that grand stage. Some of them even had supporting roles.

"Reagan and the pope," says John O'Sullivan, who wrote speeches for Margaret Thatcher, had a larger mission to "preserve and extend liberty" to Europeans and people worldwide. "That was a great moral cause," O'Sullivan declares. This was "an alliance of more than nations, more than power, more than interest." It was "an alliance of morality and decency of which Reagan and the pope were the instrument of history and Providence." It was "an alliance designed to bring about greater freedom and decency for the ordinary people living lives in Europe in particular, and around the world to a lesser extent. And it worked. It made life better. It brought about peace."

George Weigel helps put the significance of that peace in perspective: "The twentieth century was a pretty awful period in human history. Between the beginning of the First World War in 1914 and the end of the Cold War in 1991, something on the order of seventy to eighty million human beings were killed, not in war but by political violence. This is a pretty awful record. And yet the twentieth century ended with the victory of freedom in the Cold War, and the root of that victory was a revolution of conscience."

Both the pope and the president gave voice to that conscience. And, as Margaret Thatcher said, they won the Cold War without firing a shot. Anne Applebaum emphasizes the unique role of John Paul II as a religious figure. "When people talk about the pope being involved in the fall of Communism," she says, "they don't mean the pope was literally on the barricades. What they mean is that the pope gave people an alternative worldview."

The Marxist-Leninist worldview—one without God—could not stand up to the alternative that the pope presented, and that Reagan emphasized repeatedly as well. That alternative overwhelmed the barricades.

Douglas Brinkley says that Reagan sought to advance "a tide going over the world of democratic freedoms," which had been an American objective since World War II with FDR's four freedoms:

freedom of speech, freedom of worship, freedom from want, freedom from fear. Brinkley says that "the rhetoric, the language, the storyline of both the pope and Reagan" elevated them to the status of "heroes in Eastern Europe." He is quick to add that other leaders and groups played important roles as well, including Margaret Thatcher, Chancellor Helmut Kohl in West Germany, the workers of Solidarity, the Velvet Revolution of Václav Havel in Czechoslovakia, and liberation movements in Romania and Bulgaria. He also cites cultural forces, such as rock 'n' roll and jazz.

But above all stood what he calls "the fountainhead figures"—Pope John Paul II and Ronald Reagan.

James Rosebush zooms in on the two actors as evangelists for freedom, particularly religious freedom:

> They wanted to see change. Now, this is a critical thing to understand about both of these leaders: they wanted to see change and they wanted to see it happen...within the time that they felt God had given them to act. These were actors, but you have to think of the term *actor* in a broader sense. It isn't just the fact that Pope John Paul II was an actor in his youth; it isn't just the fact that Ronald Reagan was a screen actor; it was because they saw themselves as actors on the world stage effecting a change, bringing freedom to people. And why were they evangelists for freedom? Because they knew that people could only worship God if they were free. That was their objective, and that is what brought them together. It wasn't a political compact. People have to understand that. It was a spiritual compact. It was a compact to liberate anyone who was seeking freedom. And why? Because they wanted everyone to be free to worship God.

Yes, they unleashed the tide of freedom, but not freedom narrowly understood—again, not freedom as mere license. For Reagan and John Paul II, this was about both faith and freedom, those "twin beacons" that brighten the sky.

"GOD IS ULTIMATELY INVOLVED"

Both Reagan and John Paul II discerned a Divine Plan. They believed God played a role in human affairs. They said so explicitly, repeatedly.

Is Divine Providence real? People have debated the answer throughout history, and will always do so. Of course, none of us can know the complete answer to what God has planned for us. Not in this realm.

But at least some of the experts interviewed for this book observe elements of this Cold War drama that suggest a Heavenly Hand.

"You can understand how they perceived there was a Divine Plan," Stephen Kotkin remarks. "You can certainly think how improbable all of this was to come together at the same time and to come together in this particular way and with these particular figures." Kotkin notes that sometimes history seems to produce just the right person or group of persons for the time: "The historical moment somehow, someway, from somewhere, throws up a Reagan or a Thatcher or a Gorbachev or a John Paul II." Of course, human agency matters immensely. "Just because these people live in these dramatic moments doesn't mean they will live up to the call of history," Kotkin says. They can fall short, failing to seize the opportunity or to perceive the moment correctly. "This is where leadership comes in."

At the end of the Cold War, Reagan and John Paul II stood out as leaders who understood that they were living in a special moment. "Not everyone alive at the time understood this special moment," Kotkin says. The pope and the president did understand, "and they acted accordingly, rising to the occasion."

Weigel takes care in assessing the relationship between Reagan and John Paul II. He says they didn't work "quite in tandem" but rather "understood themselves to be working in parallel." The key is that "they didn't need to conspire with each other," because "they had a similar analysis of what the problem was, and I think a rather similar analysis of how Communism could be defeated."

Like Kotkin, Weigel takes note of how the pope and the president came together at a critical time in history. "How curious it is that there would be two figures of such consequence pulling on oars in the same direction as you had in President Reagan and Pope John Paul II," Weigel says. "That just doesn't happen very often.... I think it is striking that you had two men of such extraordinary quality working in a parallel way toward a great goal at the same time."

Weigel points to the confluence of circumstances that brought them together at the right time:

> You have these two figures, neither of whom was expected to rise to the eminence that they did. Neither of whom probably expected to rise to that eminence themselves. That gave both of them, when they did reach the summit of their respective professions, a profound sense of responsibility, a sense of vocation, and a sense of purpose—purpose with drive, because time is short.... Reagan was determined to restore dynamism to the United States economy and he was determined to confront Soviet power around the world. His famous statement that *my idea of the Cold War is quite simple, we win, and they lose*. John Paul II had lived a vocationally driven life since he was a young man—in the cauldron of occupied Poland, a police state where one could never be sure whether one would be alive the next day. That's a kind of pressure cooker. And out of that pressure came a vocationally purposeful young man named Karol Wojtyła who thirty-some years later would be elected bishop of Rome. That purposefulness was there in him for a long time. And what was it? It was a determination to defend the dignity of the human person against all that would demean us.

And so Karol Wojtyła and Ronald Reagan met late in each other's lives and discovered a "common purpose," Weigel says. "And the rest, as they say, is history."

Cardinal Timothy Dolan, too, comments on how rarely gifted leaders committed to freedom come together at the right moment. Dolan, a historian as well as a clergyman, points out that it happened in Europe at the end of World War II, when several leaders "believed that faith is important, that gospel values are important, that respect for religion was important." But in the 1980s, "you had that very much on steroids in Ronald Reagan and John Paul II."

Cardinal Dolan speaks confidently of a Divine Plan. "God is ultimately involved in human history," he says. "God cares about what's happening on Earth. God isn't some aloof, impersonal deity who kind of wound up the clock and let it tick when it came to creation." And one of the ways that God most fervently brings about His will, Dolan says, is in "the cultivation of wise leaders."

Bishop Robert Barron says that in seeking to fulfill God's will, we let in the light of the transcendent: "God wants us fully alive, and part of that is the awakening of our freedom to accomplish great things morally and spiritually. God wants to draw, awaken, and enhance freedom in such a way that his grace can operate more fully in the world. That's the discernment of the Divine Plan as I think both John Paul and Ronald Reagan saw it." Barron's comment recalls a line from Dante's *Divine Comedy*: "*E 'n la sua volontade è nostra pace*," which translates as "In His will is our peace."

Like others interviewed for this book, Barron sees the rise of a group of historic leaders at the end of the Cold War as more than coincidence: "God raises up great figures ... to accomplish his purposes, which is good for the world and it's good for those who God raises up. Because the more they surrender to him, the more they become themselves. Those are the theo-dynamics of this whole thing."

GREAT MEN AND GREAT WOMEN

Noting the confluence of remarkable leaders who ended the Cold War, Craig Shirley points to the "great man" theory of history.

This idea is credited to the nineteenth-century Scottish thinker Thomas Carlyle, who wrote that "the history of the world is but the biography of great men." Shirley says that "history tends to be a gentle pond, but sometimes a great man comes along and sends out the waves to radically change the direction of the future." What would have happened had Churchill not been in charge when he was? "It's hard to imagine that Neville Chamberlain could have accomplished what Winston Churchill did. It's hard to imagine that Jimmy Carter could have accomplished what Ronald Reagan did. I tend to agree that great men come along, great men who were bad or good, who alter the future."

Great men *and* great women. Shirley, like so many of those interviewed for this book, includes Margaret Thatcher in the pantheon. He says: "It is the linchpin of history that John Paul II becomes pope in 1978, Margaret Thatcher becomes prime minister in 1979, Ronald Reagan becomes president in 1981. And combined, the three of them change the course of history."

These leaders altered the course of history because, unlike their immediate predecessors, they refused to accept the Cold War division as a given. "[Many] believed that the Berlin Wall was a thing of permanence and the Soviet Union was a thing of permanence and the best thing we could do was coexist," Shirley notes. "We could contain, we could engage in détente, but they were on this earth forever and it was unalterable. Nothing could be changed."

Reagan, John Paul II, and Thatcher rejected that view. "So when Reagan is elected, they form a historic triumvirate," Shirley says. "For the first time in history, an American president is sharing classified CIA documents with the pope. Reagan appoints an envoy to the Vatican, the first time in American history, and later an ambassador to the Vatican, again, the first time in American history. He's making an ally of Pope John Paul II."

Some historians and commentators have downplayed the role of the pope and the president by suggesting that they merely superintended a Soviet collapse that would have occurred no matter what. But Shirley points out why this revisionism proves so misguided. By the late 1970s, the Soviet Union was *winning* the Cold War. The Soviets had invaded Afghanistan and had client troops in Africa. In Latin America, Nicaragua had gone Communist, El Salvador was under siege, and Cuba had been Communist since 1959. In Asia, Laos, Cambodia, and Vietnam all fell to Communism. It looked like a foregone conclusion that Soviet ideology would dominate the world, fulfilling Nikita Khrushchev's promise from two decades earlier: *We will bury you.*

But in the 1980s, all of that changed. The Berlin Wall came down. Soon thereafter the Soviet Union collapsed, the Warsaw Pact dissolved, and the Baltic states were liberated.

What happened in the intervening time, Shirley says, vindicates the great-man theory of history: "It's that history is not simply a river running down a mountain. It's that there are people who come along who build dams or divert the water or do some other thing to alter the course of that stream."

Stephen Kotkin makes a similar point. History, he says, is full of surprises and makes sense only in retrospect. "Who thought the Soviet Union was doomed in 1979 or 1980 or 1981?" he asks. "Who thought that a Polish cardinal could become pope before October 1978? Many things are just hard to imagine. And then, of course, after they happen, everybody says, 'Oh, I predicted that, or I saw that coming, or I knew that's where the future was going.' In fact, it's very hard to see the future." That's why certain leaders become so pivotal. "Some people can see this happening in real time, who can seize the moment, who can turn history in a possible direction, in part by perceiving an opportunity that history could turn in that direction. That's why we do biography. That's why we focus on certain individuals. Because these individuals are history makers by their ability, not in hindsight, not retrospectively, but in real time, to perceive these opportunities and to push history in those needed directions."

Marek Jan Chodakiewicz, who grew up in Communist Poland, attests to the fact that the "inevitable" collapse of Communism did not seem like it would ever come. He came to the United States in

1982, at age nineteen, and so he "survived a chunk of martial law in Poland," he says. "I felt Communism would collapse, but I didn't think it would happen in my lifetime. So retroactively, with 20/20 vision, you could claim, 'Oh, yes. The writing was on the wall.' It is not so."

Individuals can and do make a difference, Chodakiewicz insists: "It's only the individual who makes an effort and devotes himself, focuses on achieving a goal, who can say, 'Yes, this is what I want accomplished.'" But dedication alone will not get someone to the goal: "One must believe. One must have faith that this is the ultimate goal and that is what we can achieve. Without hope, without that drive, life is not worth living."

One needs hope and faith—two of the three theological virtues.

GENUINE ACTORS

Reflecting on the impact Ronald Reagan and John Paul II made, Cardinal Dolan returns to the fact that both men came up as actors, and emerged as actors on the world stage. Using religious language, Dolan speaks of their "charism of acting," their gift of acting, executed in a way beyond what actors typically do:

Unfortunately, we often use the term *actor* as a bit like some-body who is doing something that he or she really doesn't believe in. You are just doing it for two hours on stage. With those two men, they would see acting as, in my very care, in my very expression, in the acts that I perform that always have didactic meaning and portray something, you are por-traying your deepest sentiments and giving evidence—we would use the Christian word *witness*—to what you believe. Reagan did that... in front of the Berlin Wall.... When John Paul II could stand in front of two million people at Warsaw on his last day of those [nine] days that changed the world in June of 1979, and when he, without mentioning, without

using any political partisan vocabulary, without mentioning Russia, without mentioning Marx, without mentioning
Communism, when he could bring two million people to
chant for eleven minutes nonstop, "We want God," that's an
actor who is such a person of integrity that you are able to
bring out what is best in your audience. And boy, they both
did it with great gusto.

Genuine actors and genuine witnesses. The performances of
these two ex-actors—who, let us now concede, never really were
ex-actors—were so believable because, well, Reagan and John
Paul II believed what they said and did. They faked nothing.

These theo-historical deeds could not have been more heartfelt.
In a theo-drama, there is no separation of spiritual and stage.

ACTING WITHOUT A SCRIPT

Karol Wojtyła, on that stage at the Rhapsodic Theater, surely did
not foresee himself one day assuming the Chair of Saint Peter and
becoming one of the most consequential popes in history, helping
to win the Cold War peacefully.

Ronald Reagan, on that stage at Eureka College, surely did not
imagine himself one day assuming the Oval Office and becoming
one of the most consequential presidents in history, helping to win
the Cold War peacefully. He felt he could have been happy marry-
ing Mugs Cleaver and working at Montgomery Ward in Dixon,
Illinois.

Both men far exceeded their own expectations. Well, God had
a plan, as Nelle Reagan would have said with a wink and a smile.

Although both leaders discerned a Divine Plan, neither could
be sure whether he would see that plan fulfilled in his lifetime.
There were crosses to carry. There were struggles, doubts, conflicts.
There was the agony of wondering which, if any, evils God might
allow to persist.

In the theater of life, we don't receive the script ahead of time. Mystery always abounds.

Pope John Paul II and President Ronald Reagan endured those struggles, coped with that uncertainty, wondered at that mystery. But they felt called to their roles and acted them out with joy, even amid the uncertainty. Confident in the Divine Plan, they both lived out a mantra for which the pope became known: be not afraid.

EPILOGUE

CURTAIN CALL

On September 20, 1990, John Paul II and Ronald Reagan met for the fifth time.

Only eleven years had elapsed since Reagan had identified the pope as "the key." And only eight years had elapsed since he and the pope held their historic first meeting, when they shared their mutual conviction that God had spared their lives so that they could dedicate themselves to ending Communism's totalitarian empire.

But in that short time it had happened: the Iron Curtain had been ripped down, suddenly and spectacularly. Now the Soviet Union was coming apart, on its way to officially dissolving the next year.

The press mostly ignored this fifth meeting between John Paul II and Reagan, held at the pope's summer residence at Castel Gandolfo. By this point Reagan no longer held the presidency, having finished his second term in January 1989. The media focused mainly on Reagan's visit to the Berlin Wall earlier in his European tour, when the former president took a hammer to the forbidding barrier he had called to be torn down only three years earlier.

Although the Castel Gandolfo meeting received little attention at the time (as it has from historians since), it marked an important conclusion to the drama in which these two men played lead roles. Years later, Nancy Reagan would recall it as "a warm and wonderful meeting."[1] Mrs. Reagan said that of course the pope and her husband discussed the remarkable developments in Eastern Europe and the Soviet Union. But what stood out to her most was the personal conversation between friends.

In fact, the two men had become "best friends," according to Ronald Reagan.

Several months earlier, Reagan had welcomed some Polish visitors at his California office. During the visit he pointed to a picture of John Paul II on his office wall. "He is my best friend," Reagan told the Poles. "Yes, you know I'm Protestant, but he's still my best friend."[2]

Similarly, Nancy Reagan told Reagan adviser and biographer Martin Anderson that John Paul II was her husband's "closest friend."[3] Mrs. Reagan herself called John Paul II her "favorite" of all the many world leaders she had met.[4]

Was President Reagan merely being polite to his Polish visitors? Did Mrs. Reagan overstate the friendship between her husband and John Paul II?

It would be easy to think so. After all, the two men met only a handful of times, and it is not as if they called each other up just to catch up about their lives.

But the "best friend" designation makes perfect sense when you understand the bond that Reagan and John Paul II formed.

The pope and the president "were united by a singular bond of friendship." This apt line comes from the welcome program for a special thanksgiving Mass held for John Paul II and Ronald Reagan on June 27, 2011, at Saint Mary's Basilica in Kraków, Poland, Karol Wojtyła's home city.[5]

Bill Clark echoed this idea, more than once describing Reagan and John Paul II as "kindred spirits, kindred souls." Frank Shakespeare, who as ambassador to the Vatican knew both Reagan and John Paul II, seized on Clark's description, saying: "Yes! That's exactly what they were—kindred spirits and kindred souls."[6]

Recall, too, that Douglas Brinkley called the pope and the president "kindred spirits."

Even before they met, these kindred souls could discern shared priorities and shared conviction. But there can be no doubt that their shared suffering—the assassination attempts and similar near-death experiences, occurring only six weeks apart—"brought them closer together," to use Clark's words.

That shared suffering, together with their shared conviction about why God had spared their lives, did more than anything else to forge their "singular bond."

And so, in September 1990, these kindred spirits could reconnect and look back on how much the world had changed for the better since they first met. They would not credit themselves, though; they would credit the Divine Plan.

The fifth meeting between Reagan and John Paul II carries added poignancy because it turned out to be their last.

Four years later, Reagan announced that he had been diagnosed with Alzheimer's disease. He began what he called "the journey that will lead me into the sunset of my life."[7] Eventually he wouldn't even remember that he had been president of the United States. During this same period, the pope displayed the first signs of the Parkinson's disease that would afflict him for the rest of his life.[8]

But their singular bond endured to the end. On June 4, 2004, President George W. Bush went to the Vatican to present the pope with the Presidential Medal of Freedom. Barely able to speak, the pontiff thanked him and asked that Bush "send my regards to President Reagan and Mrs. Reagan."

Reagan died the next day.

Less than a year later, April 4, 2005, John Paul II passed away.

CONTRIBUTING A VERSE

John O'Sullivan takes stock of the "stage play" in which John Paul II and Reagan played the lead roles:

In the first act, you have everything collapsing, and you have
quite decent people who are trying to do the right thing, and
a lot of the time failing and beginning to despair. Then you
have two very remarkable people emerging to say to their own
people, first the pope to the Church, and Reagan to America:
"Look, things are not as bad as they seem. And furthermore,
this other fellow and I, and our friends like Mrs. Thatcher
and others, we know that if we go back to the basic principles
of our religion and of our nations and of human decency and
of human dignity, then we can prevail over the forces of evil
which are all too evident and don't need to be spelled out."

O'Sullivan cautions that we now need to spell out the forces
of evil we face, because people have forgotten them. So we have
begun a new act in the drama. The world we find ourselves in is in
many respects better than the one John Paul II and Ronald Reagan
operated. But life will always pose new challenges. "What we need
to do," O'Sullivan says, "is to look back to Act I."

And to what—or to whom—do we look back? O'Sullivan
responds, "I can put it no better than Mrs. Thatcher in her eulogy
to Ronald Reagan when she said: 'We have one advantage that
Ronald Reagan never had. We have *his* example.'"

Like O'Sullivan, Bishop Robert Barron emphasizes that the
human drama continues and we must act. Walt Whitman in his
poem "O Me! O Life!" ponders "the questions of these recurring,"
the ultimate question being "What good amid these [struggles and
torments], O me, O life?"

Whitman then answers his question:

That you are here—that life exists and identity,
That the powerful play goes on, and you may contribute a
    verse.

Pope John Paul II and President Ronald Reagan certainly con-
tributed their verse—"a very important verse in this powerful play,"

in Bishop Barron's words. First and foremost, Barron says, they defended freedom grounded in a transcendent truth—not freedom that can easily become dysfunctional and wicked, whether under Soviet atheistic Communism or Western secular materialism. "They spoke the truth," Barron says, "then they actively engaged in the struggle, and that's no small thing."

The Soviet empire may have landed on the ash heap of history, but the principles and values that John Paul II and Reagan advanced need to be nurtured anew.

When Saint Mary's of Kraków held the thanksgiving Mass for the lives of John Paul II and Ronald Reagan in 2011, Cardinal Stanisław Dziwisz officiated. On May 13, 1981, Dziwisz had held the wounded pope in his arms. Now he summed up the importance of the pope and the president: "This world is a battlefield of good and evil, truth and falsehood. Each of us faces a choice. Today we recall two great men who stood before this very choice, and how their decision shaped the world in which we live."

None of us knows what the Divine Plan has in store. But each of us faces a choice. Each of us may contribute a verse. The person and the act: they're inseparable.

May we, following the examples of the pope and the president, continue to choose the right actions.

NOTES

A Note on Interview Sources

Throughout this book, we cite interviews with a stellar cast who agreed to speak with Robert Orlando for his film documentary *The Divine Plan*, which serves as a companion to this book. The interview subjects include: Richard V. Allen, Anne Applebaum, Bishop Robert Barron, H.W. Brands, Douglas Brinkley, Marek Jan Chodakiewicz, Cardinal Timothy Dolan, Monika Jablonska, Stephen Kotkin, John O'Sullivan, James Rosebush, Craig Shirley, and George Weigel. Unless otherwise noted, quotations from these people come from their interviews with Orlando, held on these dates:

Richard V. Allen
National security adviser to President Reagan
August 13, 2018

Anne Applebaum
Washington Post *columnist, author of the Pulitzer Prize winner* Gulag: A History
April 10, 2018

Bishop Robert Barron
Founder of Word on Fire Catholic Ministries, auxiliary bishop of the Archdiocese of Los Angeles, author of fifteen books, and host of the PBS documentary Catholicism
April 30, 2018

H.W. Brands
Professor of history at the University of Texas at Austin, Pulitzer Prize–nominated author of thirty books
March 12, 2018

Douglas Brinkley
Presidential historian, CNN commentator, professor of history at Rice University
March 13, 2018

Marek Jan Chodakiewicz
Professor of history, Kosciuszko Chair in Polish Studies at the Institute of World Politics
April 9, 2018

Cardinal Timothy Dolan
Archbishop of New York
July 19, 2018

Monika Jablonska
Lawyer, consultant, entrepreneur, and author of Wind from Heaven
April 9, 2018

Stephen Kotkin
Professor of history and international affairs at Princeton University, author of six books on Soviet Communism
March 15, 2018

John O'Sullivan
Senior policy writer and speechwriter for Prime Minister Margaret Thatcher, former editor of National Review, *author of* The President, the Pope, and the Prime Minister
December 23, 2017

James Rosebush
Deputy assistant to President Reagan, senior White House adviser, chief of staff to First Lady Nancy Reagan, author of True Reagan
November 21, 2018

Craig Shirley
Author of four books on Ronald Reagan, including Rendezvous with Destiny *and* Last Act
May 30, 2018

George Weigel
Biographer of Pope John Paul II, distinguished senior fellow at the Ethics and Public Policy Center
November 20, 2017

PROLOGUE: TWO ACTORS IN A DIVINE PLAN

1   Douglas Brinkley, ed., *The Reagan Diaries* (New York: HarperCollins, 2007), 12.
2   Pope John Paul II, *Memory and Identity* (New York: Rizzoli, 2005), 160.
3   Cardinal Stanisław Dziwisz, *A Life with Karol* (New York: Doubleday, 2007), 133.
4   The pope later said, "I was already practically on the other side." Pope John Paul II, *Memory and Identity* (New York: Rizzoli, 2005), 161.
5   This quotation comes from Reagan's May 12, 1984, weekly radio broadcast, titled "Education," in Fred Israel, ed., *Ronald Reagan's Weekly Radio Addresses* (Wilmington, DE: Scholarly Resources Inc., 1987), 1:211.
6   Ronald Reagan, "Remarks at the National Forum on Excellence in Education," Indianapolis, Indiana, December 8, 1983.
7   Ronald Reagan, Remarks at the Annual Meeting of the American Bar Association in Atlanta, Georgia, August 1, 1983.
8   John Paul II, "Urbi et Orbi Message" (December 25, 1978), https://w2.vatican.va/content/john-paul-ii/en/messages/urbi/documents/hf_jp-ii_mes_19781225_urbi.html.

9   André Frossard and Pope John Paul II, *"Be Not Afraid!": Pope John Paul II Speaks Out on His Life, His Beliefs, and His Inspiring Vision for Humanity* (New York: St. Martin's Press, 1984), 225.

10 George Weigel, *The End and the Beginning: Pope John Paul II—The Victory of Freedom, the Last Years, the Legacy* (New York: Doubleday, 2010), 132.

11 Carl Bernstein and Marco Politi, *His Holiness: John Paul II and the Hidden History of Our Time* (New York: Doubleday, 1996), 270.

12 Pope John Paul II, *Gift and Mystery: On the Fiftieth Anniversary of My Priestly Ordination* (New York: Image, 1996), 6.

13 John Paul II, *Sollicitudo Rei Socialis* (December 30, 1987), http://w2.vatican.va/content/john-paul-ii/en/encyclicals/documents/hf_jp-ii_enc_30121987_sollicitudo-rei-socialis.html.

CHAPTER 1: THE GRAND STAGE

1   Ronald Reagan, "Remarks to the Annual National Prayer Breakfast," February 4, 1982.

2   Maureen Reagan, "A President and a Father," *Washington Times*, June 16, 2000, A23.

3   William Rose, "The Reagans and Their Pastor," *Christian Life*, May 1968, 46.

4   See: Ronald Reagan, *An American Life* (New York: Simon and Schuster, 1990), 49, 57, 70, 123.

5   Quoted in, among others, George Weigel, *Witness to Hope: The Biography of Pope John Paul II* (New York: HarperCollins, 1999), 4.

6   Edward Kosner, Karl Fleming, and William Cook, "Ronald Reagan: Rising Star in the West?" *Newsweek*, May 15, 1967, 36.

7   Bill Clark shared this sentiment with Paul Kengor many times. These include interviews done August 24, 2001, and July 17, 2003.

8   Maureen Reagan, *First Father, First Daughter: A Memoir* (New York: Little Brown Company, 1989), 279. Many Reagan staffers and family members have spoken of how Ronald Reagan believed that he was spared for a special purpose. Among many others, see: Michael Reagan with Joe Hyams, *On the Outside Looking In* (New York: Kensington Publishing, 1988), 198; Patti Davis, *Angels Don't Die: My Father's Gift of Faith* (New York: HarperCollins, 1995), 38; Bob Slosser, *Reagan Inside Out* (Waco, TX: Word Books, 1984); Kenneth Duberstein, interviewed for CNN documentary *The Reagan Years: Inside the White House*, part 2, aired February 18, 2001; Lyn Nofziger, quoted in "Reagan Officials on the March 30, 1981, Assassination Attempt," Reagan Oral History Project, http://millercenter.org/oralhistory/news/reagan-assassination-attempt; Michael Deaver, interviewed for CNN's *The Reagan Years: Inside the White House*, part 2; Michael K. Deaver, *A Different Drummer: My Thirty Years with Ronald Reagan* (New York: Harper, 2001), 151–53.

9   Brinkley, *The Reagan Diaries*, 12; Reagan, *An American Life*, 263; Edmund Morris, *Dutch: A Memoir of Ronald Reagan* (New York: Modern Library, 1999), 432.

10 See: Deaver, *A Different Drummer*, 145–47.

11 Anne Edwards, *Early Reagan: The Rise to Power* (New York: Morrow, 1987), 145–46.

12 Quoted in Helene Von Damm, *Sincerely, Ronald Reagan* (Ottawa, IL: Green Hill Publishers, 1976), 86.

13 Quoted in Von Damm, *Sincerely, Ronald Reagan*, 86.

14 Quoted in Von Damm, *Sincerely, Ronald Reagan*, 123–25.

15 Davis, *Angels Don't Die*, 48–49.

16 Quoted in Rowland Evans and Robert Novak, *The Reagan Revolution* (New York: Dutton, 1981), 208–9.

17 Whittaker Chambers, *Witness* (Washington, DC: Regnery Publishing, 1997), 85.

18 See discussion of "A Pope and a President" involving Paul Kengor, Scott Hahn, Regis

Martin, and Michael Hernon, on *Franciscan University Presents*, recorded at Franciscan University of Steubenville, first aired on EWTN, October 1, 2017.

19 On Reagan quoting Lewis, see Paul Kengor, "Ronald Reagan's Soulcraft," *American Spectator*, September 21, 2018, and Paul Kengor, *God and Ronald Reagan: A Spiritual Life* (New York: Harper, 2004), 106–7.

20 C. S. Lewis, *The Screwtape Letters: Annotated Edition* (New York: HarperOne, 2013), 48; Norman L. Geisler, *If God, Why Evil?: A New Way to Think About the Question* (Minneapolis: Bethany House, 2011), 99.

21 C. S. Lewis, *The Great Divorce* (San Francisco: HarperOne, 2001), 75; Geisler, *If God, Why Evil?*, 67.

22 Thomas C. Reeves, *America's Bishop: The Life and Times of Fulton J. Sheen* (San Francisco: Encounter Books, 2001), 155.

23 See: Peter Kreeft, "Freewill and Predestination," posted at http://www.peterkreeft.com/topics-more/freewill-predestination.htm.

24 Ibid.

25 Ibid.

26 Address of John Paul II to the Fiftieth General Assembly of the United Nations Organization, October 5, 1995.

27 From his presidential years, see (among others): Reagan, "Remarks at the First Annual Commemoration of the Days of Remembrance of Victims of the Holocaust," April 30, 1981; Reagan, "Address at Commencement Exercises at the United States Military Academy," May 27, 1981; and Reagan, "Remarks at Eureka College," February 6, 1984.

28 Reagan, "America the Beautiful," commencement address, William Woods College, June 1952.

29 Reagan, "Remarks at the Annual Convention of the National Religious Broadcasters," January 31, 1983.

CHAPTER 2: THE ACTING PERSONS

1 Quoted in Monika Jablonska, *Wind from Heaven: John Paul II—The Poet Who Became Pope* (Kettering, OH: Angelico Press, 2017), 71.

2 See 1 Thess 1:6–7; 1 Thess 2:14; 1 Cor 4:16; 1 Cor 11:1, Phil 3:17, and Phil 2:5–11.

3 Quoted in Daniel McInerny, "John Paul II—Subversive Actor," *Catholic World Report*, April 24, 2014, https://www.catholicworldreport.com/2014/04/24/john-paul-ii-subversive-actor/.

4 Ibid.

5 Robert Barron, *Thomas Aquinas: Spiritual Master* (New York: The Crossroad Publishing Company, 2008), 148, 151–53.

6 Barron, *Thomas Aquinas: Spiritual Master*, 173, 184.

7 Thomas Rourke, "Personalism," in Michael L. Coulter, Stephen M. Krason, et al., eds., *Encyclopedia of Catholic Social Thought, Social Science, and Social Policy* (Lanham, MD: Scarecrow Press, 2007), 801–3.

8 Avery Dulles, "John Paul II and the Mystery of the Human Person," *America Magazine*, February 2, 2004.

9 Weigel, *Witness to Hope*, 175–76.

10 Quoted in Dulles, "John Paul II and the Mystery of the Human Person."

11 Ibid.

12 Weigel, *Witness to Hope*, 172–75.

13 According to the *Encyclopedia of Catholic Social Thought, Social Science, and Social Policy*: "What is phenomenology? It would be most accurate to identify it as a philosophical movement rather than a philosophy.... Given its rather loose and amorphous nature, it

is virtually impossible to come up with anything like a precise definition of phenomenology, or, for that matter, with even a description of it which would be fully satisfactory to all those who would be prepared to call themselves phenomenologists." See D. Q. McInerny, "Phenomenology," in Coulter, Krason, et al., eds., *Encyclopedia of Catholic Social Thought, Social Science, and Social Policy.*

14 Weigel, *Witness to Hope*, 127.

15 Ibid., 27.

16 Ibid., 7, 14.

17 Ibid., 172–75.

18 Ibid., 172–73.

19 Rocco Buttiglione, *Karol Wojtyła: The Thought of the Man Who Became Pope John Paul II* (Grand Rapids, MI: Wm. B. Eerdmans Publishing, 1997), 82.

20 Douglas Flippen, "Was John Paul II a Thomist or a Phenomenologist?" *Faith and Reason* (Spring 2006): 65–106, https://www.catholicculture.org/culture/library/view.cfm?recnum=8105.

21 Weigel, *Witness to Hope*, 126.

22 Ibid., 175.

23 Richard A. Spinello, *The Genius of John Paul II: The Great Pope's Moral Wisdom* (Lanham, MD: Sheed & Ward, 2007), 90–92.

24 Weigel, *Witness to Hope*, 175–76.

25 John Paul II, *Redemptor Hominis* (March 4, 1979), http://w2.vatican.va/content/john-paul-ii/en/encyclicals/documents/hf_jp-ii_enc_04031979_redemptor-hominis.html.

26 Pope John Paul II, *Veritatis Splendor*, section 54 (August 6, 1993), http://w2.vatican.va/content/john-paul-ii/en/encyclicals/documents/hf_jp-ii_enc_06081993_veritatis-splendor.html.

27 Spinello, *The Genius of John Paul II*, 97, 117.

28 Quoted in Weigel, *Witness to Hope*, 127.

29 Reagan, "Remarks at Georgetown University's Bicentennial Convocation," October 1, 1988.

30 Martin and Annelise Anderson, in their careful research of the declassified material from this period, estimate that by the end of 1981 Reagan and John Paul II had exchanged "a dozen or so" letters. Some were sent by cable, others delivered directly. "The letters from the Vatican," the Andersons write, "were beautifully written on thick embossed paper; Reagan's letters were not quite as elegant, but just as clear and direct as the Pope's in spelling out his intentions." The Andersons note the significance of this rich correspondence: "By early 1982, many months before Reagan would meet the Pope in person, the tone of their relations had been set by these letters." Martin and Annelise Anderson, *Reagan's Secret War: The Untold Story of His Fight to Save the World from Nuclear Disaster* (New York: Crown, 2009), 90.

31 Lee Edwards, *Just Right: A Life in Pursuit of Liberty* (Wilmington, DE: ISI Books, 2017), 144–45.

32 For a detailed breakdown of this speech, see Kengor, *God and Ronald Reagan*, 233–70.

33 Reagan was, in effect, a full coauthor of this speech, along with his devoted Catholic chief speechwriter, Tony Dolan. Dolan wrote the line on the phenomenology of evil, which Reagan retained, as opposed to numerous other lines in the address that Reagan crossed out. In fact, Reagan deleted the first half of the sentence but kept "phenomenology of evil." See the original marked-up draft of the speech in Paul Kengor, *11 Principles of a Reagan Conservative* (New York: Beaufort Books, 2014), 115–33 (for precise section, see page 126).

34 The press conference was held January 29, 1981.

CHAPTER 3: ENTRANCES

1 Ronald Reagan, *Where's the Rest of Me?* (New York: Duell, Sloan and Pearce, 1965).

2 John Paul II, homily in Wadowice, Poland, June 16, 1999, as quoted by Jablonska, *Wind from Heaven*, 61.

3 See, among others, Jason Evert, "John Paul II and the Blessed Sacrament," *Catholic World Report*, April 18, 2014; and Francis Phillips, "Saint John Paul II's Father Is a Role Model for All Men," *Catholic Herald*, June 16, 2014.

4 Pope John Paul II, *Gift and Mystery*, 9–22.

5 See Brands discussing this in a June 5, 2015, presentation on C-SPAN 2's Book TV, https://www.c-span.org/video/?328703-2/hw-brands-reagan.

6 Information provided by the Reagan Library, document titled "Residences of Ronald Reagan."

7 The source for this is literature provided by the Reagan Boyhood Home, 816 South Hennepin Avenue, Dixon, Illinois.

8 Patti Davis interviewed on television documentary *Ronald Reagan: A Legacy Remembered*, History Channel, 2002.

9 Kengor, *God and Ronald Reagan*, chapters 1–3, and especially pages 17–26.

10 Rosebush also recounts this episode in his book *True Reagan: What Made Ronald Reagan Great and Why It Matters* (New York: Center Street, 2017), 143–44.

11 Peggy Noonan, *John Paul the Great* (New York: Viking, 2005), 129.

12 Tad Szulc, *Pope John Paul II: The Biography* (New York: Gallery Books, 1988), 117; Noonan, *John Paul the Great*, 130; Weigel, *Witness to Hope*, 68.

13 H.W. Brands, *Reagan: The Life*, (New York: Doubleday, 2015), 42.

14 Reagan, *Where's the Rest of Me?* 99; Maureen Reagan, *First Father, First Daughter*, 61; and Morris, *Dutch*, 12.

15 Weigel, *Witness to Hope*, 37.

16 Father Peter John Cameron, "Pope John Paul II, Playwright Saint," *National Catholic Register*, April 20, 2014.

17 Buttiglione, *Karol Wojtyła*, 21–22.

18 See information compiled by the Ronald Reagan Society of Eureka College compiled, https://reagan.eureka.edu/visit-reagans-campus.html.

19 Kengor, *God and Ronald Reagan*, 28–31.

20 Garry Wills, *Reagan's America: Innocents at Home* (Garden City, NY: Doubleday, 1987), 27.

21 "Cantatas Sung by Dixon Choirs Sunday Evening," *Dixon Telegraph*, December 22, 1924.

22 "Annual Meeting and Supper for Christian Church Last Eve," *Dixon Telegraph*, January 15, 1925.

23 "Program in Tampico Most Enjoyable," *Dixon Telegraph*, August 1, 1925.

24 Buttiglione, *Karol Wojtyła*, 22–23.

25 Weigel, *Witness to Hope*, 63–64.

26 Buttiglione, *Karol Wojtyła*, 17, 19–20.

27 Jablonska, *Wind from Heaven*, 129–30.

28 Ibid., 143–44.

29 Ibid., 143.

30 Karol Wojtyła, "Our God's Brother," in *The Collected Plays and Writings on Theater* (Berkeley, CA: University of California Press, 1987), 188.

31 Cameron, "Pope John Paul II, Playwright Saint."

32 Jablonska, *Wind from Heaven*, 135.

33 Ibid., 138.

34 Cameron, "Pope John Paul II, Playwright Saint."

35 Juliusz Słowacki, "The Slavic Pope," in *Poems*, vol. 1 (Wrocław: Ossoliński, 1959), 250–51.

36 Buttiglione, *Karol Wojtyła*, 23, 29.

37 Joan Frances Gormley, *John of Avila: Audi, Filia* (New York: Paulist Press, 2006), 98–99.

38 Ibid., 98–99.

39 C. S. Lewis, *The Problem of Pain* (New York: Macmillan, 1962), 93.

40 See Kengor, *God and Ronald Reagan*, 32–40.

41 Morris, *Dutch*, 249.

42 Bob Colacello, "Ronnie and Nancy," *Vanity Fair*, August 2004, https://www.vanityfair.com/news/2004/08/reagans200408.

43 See Kengor, *God and Ronald Reagan*, 1–16, 27–40.

CHAPTER 4: TRANSITIONS

1   Reagan, *Where's the Rest of Me?* 162.

2   John Howard Lawson, *Film in the Battle of Ideas* (New York: Masses & Mainstream, 1953).

3   Peter Hanson, *Dalton Trumbo, Hollywood Rebel: A Critical Survey and Filmography* (Jefferson, NC: McFarland, 2001), 79.

4   Paul Kengor, *The Crusader: Ronald Reagan and the Fall of Communism* (New York: HarperCollins, 2006), 10–12.

5   James Mann, *The Rebellion of Ronald Reagan* (New York: Penguin Group, 2009), 18.

6   Reagan performed at the Last Frontier in February 1954. Later in 1954, he began the GE job. Information on Reagan at the Last Frontier came from the hotel, which is now called the New Frontier; the name has changed a number of times.

7   "Annual TV Sales, 1939–1959," http://www.tvhistory.tv/Annual_TV_Sales_39-59.JPG.

8   See: Morris, *Dutch*, 304.

9   Nancy Reagan speaking in an interview on "Reagan," *The American Experience*. She gives a number of other examples in her 1980 autobiography. See: Nancy Reagan, *Nancy* (New York: Morrow, 1980), 143.

10 Reagan, *An American Life*, 49, 57, 70, 123.

11 Lou Cannon, "Actor, Governor, President, Icon," *Washington Post*, June 6, 2004.

12 "Jane Wyman Divorced; Blames Rift on Politics," *Los Angeles Times*, June 29, 1948.

13 Thomas W. Evans, *The Education of Ronald Reagan: The General Electric Years and the Untold Story of His Conversion to Conservatism* (New York: Columbia University Press, 2006), 4.

14 Ibid., 4.

15 Paul Kengor, *A Pope and a President* (Wilmington, DE: ISI Books, 2017), 128.

16 William Rose, "The Reagans and Their Pastor," *Christian Life*, May 1968, 43–44.

17 Ibid., 43–44.

18 The Broder piece is cited and quoted in Lou Cannon, *Ronnie and Jesse: A Political Odyssey* (Garden City, NY: Doubleday, 1969), 266.

19 Quoted in Rowland Evans and Robert Novak, *The Reagan Revolution* (New York: Dutton, 1981), 208–9.

20 Maureen Reagan, "A President and a Father," *Washington Times*, June 16, 2000, A23.

21 Neva Waggoner, *Richly Blessed* (Phoenix, AZ: Imperial, 1989), 149.

CHAPTER 5: "BE NOT AFRAID"

1   "New Head of the Catholic Church," *Current Digest of the Soviet Press* 30, no. 42 (November 15, 1978): 20.

2   Weigel, *Witness to Hope*, 279.

3   Roger Boyes and John Moody, *Messenger of the Truth* (Warsaw: Drukarnia Loretanska, 2013), 48. This book was originally published by Boyes and Moody as *The Priest and the Policeman* (New York: Summit Books, 1987). Boyes updated the 2013 version.

4 Carl Bernstein and Marco Politi, *His Holiness: John Paul II and the Hidden History of Our Time* (New York: Doubleday, 1996), 174–75.

5 Christopher Andrew and Vasili Mitrokhin, *The Sword and the Shield: The Mitrokhin Archive and the Secret History of the KGB* (New York: Basic Books, 1999), 512.

6 "Homily of His Holiness John Paul II," Holy Mass, Victory Square, Warsaw, Poland, June 2, 1979. Transcript taken from official Vatican website: https://w2.vatican.va/content/john-paul-ii/en/homilies/1979/documents/hf_jp-ii_hom_19790602_polonia-varsavia.html. Retrieved November 4, 2015.

7 "Narrator's Preface," in Dziwisz, *A Life with Karol*.

8 Noonan, *John Paul the Great*, 25.

CHAPTER 6: THE PAPAL STAGE AND THE PRESIDENTIAL STAGE

1 For this account we draw on several sources, all of them from Richard V. Allen, and all consistent. In addition to the interview Allen gave for this book, we refer to: Allen, "Pope John Paul II, Ronald Reagan, and the Collapse of Communism: An Historic Confluence," in Douglas E. Streusand, Norman A. Bailey, and Francis H. Marlo, eds., *The Grand Strategy That Won the Cold War: Architecture of Triumph* (Lanham, MD: Lexington Books, 2016); Allen in Peter Schweizer, ed., *The Fall of the Berlin Wall: Reassessing the Causes and Consequences of the End of the Cold War* (Stanford, CA: Hoover Institution Press, 2000), 55–56; and Allen in Peter Hannaford, ed., *Recollections of Reagan* (New York: William Morrow, 1997), 6–8.

2 Allen, in Schweizer, ed., *The Fall of the Berlin Wall*, 55–56.

3 Allen, "Pope John Paul II, Ronald Reagan, and the Collapse of Communism: An Historic Confluence," in Streusand, Bailey, and Marlo, eds., *The Grand Strategy That Won the Cold War*.

4 Paul Kengor, interview with Richard V. Allen, November 12, 2001; and Richard Allen, "An Extraordinary Man in Extraordinary Times: Ronald Reagan's Leadership and the Decision to End the Cold War," address to the Hoover Institution and the William J. Casey Institute of the Center for Security Policy, Washington, DC, February 22, 1999, text printed in Schweizer, ed., *The Fall of the Berlin Wall*, 52.

5 Located in "Ronald Reagan: Pre-Presidential Papers: Selected Radio Broadcasts, 1975–1979," October 31, 1978, to October 1979, Box 4, RRL. For a full transcript, see: Kiron K. Skinner, Annelise Anderson, and Martin Anderson, eds., *Reagan, In His Own Hand: The Writings of Ronald Reagan that Reveal His Revolutionary Vision for America* (New York: Free Press, 2001), 176–77.

6 Paul Kengor, interview with Bill Clark, August 24, 2001.

7 Editorial, "The Polish Pope in Poland," *New York Times*, June 5, 1979, A20.

8 Noonan, *John Paul the Great*, 30.

CHAPTER 7: THE BULLETS OF SPRING 1981

1 Lawrence Altman, "Doctor Says President Lost More Blood Than Disclosed," *New York Times*, April 3, 1981.

2 Weigel, *Witness to Hope*, 413.

3 "Remarks by Secretary of State Alexander M. Haig Jr. About the Attempted Assassination of the President," *Public Papers of the Presidents of the United States: Ronald Reagan*, March 30, 1981.

4 Lawrence K. Altman, "The Doctor's World: After Assassination Attempts, Those Unreliable Early Reports," *New York Times*, June 2, 1981.

5 Weigel, *Witness to Hope*, 413; André Frossard and Pope John Paul II, *"Be Not Afraid!":*

Pope John Paul II Speaks Out on His Life, His Beliefs, and His Inspiring Vision for Humanity
(New York: St. Martin's Press, 1984), 225.

6   George Weigel, *The End and the Beginning: Pope John Paul II—The Victory of Freedom, the
     Last Years, the Legacy* (New York: Doubleday, 2010), 132.

7   Altman, "The Doctor's World"; John Paul II, *Memory and Identity*, 161.

8   Brinkley, *The Reagan Diaries*, 12.

9   Maureen Reagan, *First Father, First Daughter*, 279; Michael Reagan with Joe Hyams,
     On the Outside Looking In, 198; Slosser, *Reagan Inside Out*; Duberstein, interviewed for
     CNN documentary *The Reagan Years: Inside the White House*, part 2; Nofziger, quoted in
     "Reagan Officials on the March 30, 1981, Assassination Attempt."

10   Brinkley, *The Reagan Diaries*, 12.

11   Reagan, *An American Life*, 269.

12   Michael Deaver, interviewed for CNN's *The Reagan Years: Inside the White House*, part 2.
     See also: Deaver, *A Different Drummer*, 151–53.

13   Reagan, Letter to Leonid Brezhnev, April 24, 1981, http://www.thereaganfiles.
     com/19810424-2.pdf.

14   Deaver, *A Different Drummer*, 145–47.

15   Laurence I. Barrett, *Gambling with History: Ronald Reagan in the White House* (New
     York: Doubleday, 1983), 124; and Deaver, *A Different Drummer*, 114.

16   Brinkley, *The Reagan Diaries*, 23, 317, 419.

17   John Paul II, *Memory and Identity*, 160.

18   Ibid., 161.

19   Frossard and Pope John Paul II, *"Be Not Afraid!,"* 251.

20   Pope John Paul II, Angelus message on the Solemnity of the Assumption of the Blessed
     Virgin Mary, Castel Gandolfo, August 15, 2003.

21   Interestingly, Ronald Reagan discussed Fátima and its potential connection to the assas-
     sination attempt on John Paul II with close aides and probably with the pope himself.
     Frank Shakespeare, who served as U.S. ambassador to the Vatican, told Paul Kengor that
     he briefed Reagan at length on Fátima just before the president's June 1987 meeting with
     the pope. Shakespeare reported that Reagan, a non-Catholic, "listened very, very care-
     fully—very intently," adding, "He was *very* interested." The former ambassador also said
     that John Paul II "very clearly" would have spoken to Reagan about Fátima during one of
     their meetings. Shakespeare explained: "At some point, the pope would have said to Rea-
     gan: 'For anyone to talk to me in depth about foreign policy, about Russia, about the Cold
     War, they will need to understand my thinking and relationship to Mary and also Mary's
     appearance at Fátima and the whole relationship between Mary and Russia and the Cold
     War.'" Paul Kengor, interview with Frank Shakespeare, March 5, 2013. For a much more
     detailed discussion of Reagan, John Paul II, and the Fátima connection, see Kengor, *A
     Pope and a President*, especially ch. 1, "An Echo," and ch. 32, "Reagan's Fátima Briefing."

22   Dziwisz, *A Life with Karol*, 135.

23   Ibid., 136.

24   Ibid.

25   Ibid.

26   Pope John Paul II, *Memory and Identity*, 163.

27   Reagan's words are printed on a White House Situation Room cable, today housed at
     the Reagan Library. Titled "Reply to Get-Well Message from Pope to President," the
     document bears the date "05/25/81" on top, but the White House seems to have sent
     it to the Vatican sometime earlier in May 1981. Interestingly, the cable states that the
     "White House has no record of actual receipt" of a get-well message from the pope, even
     though such a message had been printed in the official Vatican newspaper, *L'Osservatore
     Romano*. Even if there was a failure in direct delivery to the White House, the Reagan
     team made sure that the president responded with his appreciation.

28   The text of this message is likewise printed in a "05/25/81" White House Situation Room

cable held at the Reagan Library. The official Reagan Library file citation is: Executive Secretariat (ES), National Security Council (NSC), Head of State File (HSF): Records, Vatican: Pope John Paul II, Ronald Reagan Library, Box 41, Folder "Cables 1 of 2."

29   Allen, "Pope John Paul II, Ronald Reagan, and the Collapse of Communism."

30   The letter, prefaced by a May 22, 1981, White House memo from Mort Allin to Larry Speakes (both of the White House press office), is held at the Reagan Library.

31   The term *theo-drama* is credited to Catholic theologian Hans Urs von Balthasar, first published in German as *Theodramatik*. In the preface to volume 1 of the five-part work, Balthasar writes: "The model of the theatre is a more promising point of departure for a study of *theo-drama* than man's secular, social activity. For in the theatre man attempts a kind of transcendence, endeavoring both to observe and to judge his own truth, in virtue of a transformation...by which he tries to gain clarity about himself." Hans Urs von Balthasar, *Theo-Drama: Theological Dramatic Theory, Vol. 1: Prolegomena* (San Francisco: Ignatius Press, 1988), 11–12, translation by Graham Harrison.

CHAPTER 8: "HOW PROVIDENCE INTERVENED"

1   Alex Alexiev, "The Kremlin and the Pope," *The Rand Paper Series* (The Rand Corporation, Santa Monica, CA), April 1983, 12–13.

2   Ibid., 13.

3   Bob Woodward, *Veil: The Secret Wars of the CIA, 1981–1987* (New York: Simon and Schuster, 1987), 102.

4   Bill Clark interview with Raymond Arroyo, *The World Over*, EWTN, initially recorded at the Clark ranch in Shandon, California, in 2008.

5   See discussion in Kengor, *A Pope and a President*, 273–77.

6   Kengor, *A Pope and a President*, 277.

7   Quoted in Bernstein and Politi, *His Holiness*, 355.

8   It is not clear where Brinkley encountered this assessment from Reagan, though one can presume he saw it in Reagan's diaries, which he edited. The published version of *The Reagan Diaries* includes sixteen references to John Paul II and four to Mother Teresa, in which Reagan expresses his admiration for and even awe of both of them. He writes of John Paul II, "He's truly a great man." Brinkley, *The Reagan Diaries*, 529.

9   Clark interview with Arroyo, *The World Over*. Clark said this to Paul Kengor many times.

10   Paul Kengor email correspondence with Robert Reilly, September 3, 2015.

11   Clark interview with Arroyo.

12   Quoted in Schweizer, *Reagan's War*, 213.

13   Carl Bernstein, "The Holy Alliance," *Time*, February 24, 1992, 28–35.

14   Ibid., 29–31.

15   Bill Clark, "President Reagan and the Wall," Address to the Council of National Policy, San Francisco, California, March 2000, 7–8.

16   Quoted in Bernstein, "The Holy Alliance."

17   President Ronald Reagan, "Remarks Following a Meeting with Pope John Paul II in Vatican City," June 7, 1982.

18   Aleksandr Bovin, "A Face Not a Policy," *Izvestia*, January 10, 1982, 5, published as "Bovin on U.S. Poland Policy," in *FBIS*, FBIS-SOV-10-JAN-82, January 10, 1982, F5. See also: Vitaly Korionov, "Production Line of Crimes and Hypocrisy," *Pravda*, January 10, 1984, published as "'Unprecedented Wave' of Lies Seen in U.S.," in *FBIS*, FBIS-SOV-13-JAN-84, January 13, 1984, A4.

19   Reagan, "Remarks Following a Meeting with Pope John Paul II in Vatican City."

20   The historian for Reagan's childhood church says, "The general opinion was that [Reagan's brother] Neil was the actor and Ronald was the minister type." See: Kengor, *God and Ronald Reagan*, 31–32.

21 See Kengor, *A Pope and a President*, 590–91n56.

22 Carl Bernstein and Marco Politi report that the total reached roughly $50 million over six to seven years. Peter Schweizer reported $8 million annually. Other estimates seem close to these. See: Bernstein and Politi, *His Holiness*, 357; and Schweizer, *Victory*, 75–76. A book by Seth Jones reports that the CIA spent less than $20 million between 1983 and 1991 to aid Solidarity. See: Seth G. Jones, *A Covert Action: Reagan, the CIA, and the Cold War Struggle in Poland* (New York and London: W.W. Norton & Company, 2018), 10, 297, 301, 304.

23 Robert M. Gates, *From the Shadows: The Ultimate Insider's Story of Five Presidents and How They Won the Cold War* (New York: Simon and Schuster, 1996).

24 For decades, rumors have circulated that Wałęsa served as a Communist spy in the 1970s. In 2008 two Polish historians published a book presenting evidence that the labor leader served as a paid informant for the Communist secret police. And in 2016 Poland's Institute of National Remembrance said that documents seized from the home of a former Communist-era interior minister, General Czesław Kiszczak, offered further evidence of Wałęsa's spying. Wałęsa has long denied the allegations, saying that he never took money from the Communists and that he spoke with Poland's secret services only as part of his labor union activities. See: " 'Positive Proof' Lech Walesa Was a Communist Spy: Interview with Historian Slawomir Cenckiewicz," *Der Spiegel*, June 23, 2008, https://www.spiegel.de/international/europe/interview-with-historian-slawomir-cenckiewicz-positive-proof-lech-walesa-was-a-communist-spy-a-561414. html; "Lech Walesa 'Was Paid Communist Informant,' " BBC News, February 18, 2016, https://www.bbc.com/news/world-europe-35602437; "Lech Wałęsa: I Was Not an Agent of the Polish Security Services," *The Guardian*, March 10, 2016, https://www. theguardian.com/world/2016/mar/10/lech-waesa-not-agent-spy-polish-security-services-interview.

25 Thomas A. Sancton, "Poland: Back to the Precipice," *Time*, April 6, 1981, http://content. time.com/time/magazine/article/0,9171,951623,00.html.

26 See: Andrew and Mitrokhin, *The Sword and the Shield*, 521.

27 Weigel, *The End and the Beginning*, 129.

28 Many primary-source records, eyewitness accounts, intelligence reports, and historical accounts suggest that the Soviets were preparing to invade Poland in March 1981, only to pull back suddenly. For a detailed account of that period and a theory as to why the Soviets did not invade (did it have to do with the assassination attempt on Ronald Reagan?), see Kengor, *A Pope and a President*, ch. 17, "The Soviet Invasion That Wasn't."

CHAPTER 9: CODE NAME: CAPPUCCINO

1 Bernstein, "The Holy Alliance."

2 One source who worked at the nunciature as a teenager at the time told Paul Kengor that the coffee was actually espresso rather than cappuccino, as no self-respecting Italian (Laghi) would serve cappuccino in the afternoon. Clark, a rancher from California, was unfamiliar with the distinctions.

3 See: Bernstein, "The Holy Alliance."

4 Among other occasions, see Clark's interview with Arroyo, *The World Over*. EWTN has rebroadcast the original several times, including in the weeks after Clark's death in August 2013.

5 Herb Meyer speaking at the Third Annual Ronald Reagan Lecture Series, Grove City College, Grove City, Pennsylvania, February 5, 2009. Meyer reaffirmed this to Paul Kengor in an August 28, 2015, email: "As I said, he figured that God had given him one last shot and he wasn't going to waste it. And he didn't."

6 Bernstein, "The Holy Alliance."

7   Vernon Walters, *The Mighty and the Meek: Dispatches from the Front Line of Diplomacy* (London: St. Ermin's Press, 2001), 232.

8   Ibid., 232–33.

9   See: Bernstein, "The Holy Alliance," and Bernstein and Politi, *His Holiness*, 21–22.

10   Quoted in Malachi Martin, *The Keys of This Blood: The Struggle for World Dominion Between Pope John Paul II, Mikhail Gorbachev, and the Capitalist West* (New York: Touchstone, 1990), 120.

11   Bernstein, "The Holy Alliance."

12   Paul Kengor, interview with Owen Smith, December 30, 2005.

13   See: *Wolf Blitzer Reports*, CNN, April 7, 2005, transcript at http://www.cnn.com/TRANSCRIPTS/0504/07/wbr.01.html.

14   See Robert Gates's speech for a centennial remembrance of Ronald Reagan, delivered May 24, 2011, at the Ronald Reagan Building in Washington, http://archive.defense.gov/speeches/speech.aspx?speechid=1571.

15   Benjamin Weiser, *A Secret Life: The Polish Officer, His Covert Mission, and the Price He Paid to Save His Country* (New York: PublicAffairs, 2004), 3. Paul Kengor also learned of Kukliński's importance from Gus Weiss, who said only vaguely that Kukliński "earned his salary during the crisis." Paul Kengor, interview with Weiss, November 26, 2002.

16   See the official Kukliński website in English, specifically this page: http://www.kuklinski.us/page11.htm.

17   See: Kengor, *The Crusader*, 92–93, and Kengor, *A Pope and a President*, 234, 271.

CHAPTER 10: THE SOVIET HAND AT WORK

1   Clark discussion with Paul Kengor.

2   This investigation is a central theme of Paul Kengor's book *A Pope and a President*. See, in particular, ch. 29, titled, "The Russians Did It."

3   John Koehler, *Spies in the Vatican* (New York: Pegasus Books, 2009), 87–88.

4   Ibid., 87–88.

5   Ibid.

6   Weigel said this in his interview for this book. Similarly, in *The End and the Beginning*, his sequel to *Witness to Hope*, he wrote, "Contrary to some reports, the Central Committee decree did not order the assassination of John Paul II." He said that the committee "was an administrative body that lacked the competence to order such measures."

7   Gorbachev interview with *Il Tempo*, January 20, 2000, as quoted in Koehler, *Spies in the Vatican*, 88–89.

8   Koehler, *Spies in the Vatican*, 62–64.

9   Michael Wines, "Upheaval in the East: 1980 Soviet Defector Emerges with Account of KGB Plots," *New York Times*, March 3, 1990.

10   See, among others, Philip Pullella, "Soviet Union Ordered Pope Shooting: Italy Commission," Reuters, March 2, 2006; Edward Pentin, "Bombshell Claim: Soviets Wanted Pope Killed," *National Catholic Register*, March 12–18, 2006, A1.

11   In 2006, Paul Kengor discovered this speech draft while working on a biography of Clark. Kengor found the document while digging through old boxes of material from Clark's years in the Reagan administration.

12   See the discussion of this in Kengor, *A Pope and a President*, 532, 542, and in the new afterword to the 2018 paperback edition of *A Pope and a President*.

13   Thomas P. Melady, "John Paul II Rejected Assassination Inquiry," *National Catholic Reporter*, April 29, 2005.

CHAPTER 11: "IT IS GOD'S WILL"

1   Mikhail Gorbachev, *Memoirs* (New York: Doubleday, 1995), 457.
2   Weigel, *Witness to Hope*, 604–5.
3   Enzio Mauro and Paolo Mieli, "'He Is a Man of Integrity,' Pontiff Says of Gorbachev," *La Stampa*, March 9, 1992.
4   Weigel, *Witness to Hope*, 604–5.
5   Casaroli told this to Thomas Melady, U.S. ambassador to the Holy See from 1989 to 1993 under President George H. W. Bush. See: Melady, "John Paul II Rejected Assassination Inquiry." See also: Gorbachev, *Memoirs*, 508; Tad Szulc, "Principled Allies: Gorbachev and the Pope," *Newsweek*, April 10, 1995.
6   Gorbachev, *Memoirs*, 508; Tad Szulc, "Principled Allies: Gorbachev and the Pope."
7   Deaver, *A Different Drummer*, 118.
8   Mauro and Mieli, "'He Is a Man of Integrity,' Pontiff Says of Gorbachev."
9   See Paul Kengor, "A World of Fewer Nuclear Weapons: Ronald Reagan's Willingness to Negotiate," in Jeffrey L. Chidester and Paul Kengor, eds., *Reagan's Legacy in a World Transformed* (Cambridge: Harvard University Press, 2015).
10 Kengor, "A World of Fewer Nuclear Weapons."
11 James Mann, *The Rebellion of Ronald Reagan: A History of the End of the Cold War* (New York: Viking Penguin, 2009), xvi.
12 Stephen Kotkin, *Armageddon Averted: The Soviet Collapse, 1970–2000* (New York: Oxford University Press, 2008).
13 See the discussion in Kengor, *The Crusader*, 219–23.
14 John O'Sullivan, *The President, the Pope, and the Prime Minister: Three Who Changed the World* (Washington, DC: Regnery, 2006), 4–5.
15 For more on this moment, see: Kengor, *A Pope and a President*, 489–90.
16 Weigel, *Witness to Hope*, 227.
17 See: Kengor, *The Crusader*, 263–67.
18 Reagan, "Address to the Cambridge Union Society," Cambridge, England, December 5, 1990, quoted in Frederick J. Ryan Jr., ed., *Ronald Reagan: The Wisdom and Humor of the Great Communicator* (San Francisco: Collins, 1995).

CHAPTER 12: "I DIDN'T BRING THE WALL DOWN"

1   Clark shared this story in an interview with Paul Kengor, August 24, 2001. He also told the story in a speech to a group in Washington on February 22, 1999. In that speech the admirer congratulated Reagan for "your success in ending the Cold War." Clark did not hesitate to tell this nonreligious audience that he saw Reagan smile and reply confidently, "No, not my success but a team effort by Divine Providence." For a transcript, see: Clark in Schweizer, ed., *The Fall of the Berlin Wall*, 75.
2   Paul Kengor, interview with Clark, August 24, 2001.
3   Paul Kengor, interview with Richard V. Allen, November 12, 2001.
4   Reagan, "Democracy's Next Battle," remarks to Oxford Union Society, Oxford, England, December 4, 1992. The quotation comes from Winston Churchill, Speech at Harrow School, October 29, 1941, https://www.nationalchurchillmuseum.org/never-give-in-never-never-never.html.
5   Bernstein and Politi, *His Holiness*, 356.

EPILOGUE: CURTAIN CALL

1   See Kengor, *A Pope and a President*, 496.

2   Paul Kengor, interview with Chris M. Zawitkowski, November 9, 2005.

3   Mary Claire Kendall heard this from Martin Anderson in June 2009 when Anderson was speaking at the Heritage Foundation regarding his book *Reagan's Secret War*. Kendall reported on it at the time in an article for *The Wanderer*, "Reagan Revisited," August 6, 2009. She also wrote about it in "Seeing the Duke in a Whole New Light," Breitbart. com, June 11, 2009. Paul Kengor confirmed this with Kendall in email exchanges on November 24–25, 2015. Kengor followed up by emailing Annelise Anderson, Martin's spouse and coauthor, for confirmation on November 27, 2015. (Martin Anderson had since passed away.) Annelise responded with an email on December 9, 2015, in which she confirmed: "I remember the event—Martin and I were both there. And we talked to Mary Claire afterward, as well. I think Mary Claire's article is an accurate reflection of her (Mary's) conversation, or interview, with Martin." Annelise did, however, add a caveat: "I think 'close friends' is not a good description of the relationship.... RR and JPII were not 'pals' in the sense of friends who get together and talk about 'stuff.' My guess is that neither one of them had friends of that type. They were both too busy." But she noted some of the many commonalities between the two men and added, "There's enough here of interest without getting into the question of what it means to be a 'friend' and what 'closest' means." Precisely. The key point is that they shared unique bonds and were united in a pursuit of an objective of supreme importance, politically, historically, and spiritually.

4   Email correspondence with Joanne Drake, Mrs. Reagan's longtime personal assistant, August 29, 2012, following conversations with her and her conversations with Mrs. Reagan, all held in August 2012. Mrs. Reagan pointed this out more than once.

5   Joanne Drake attended the Mass. All information quoted here comes from the materials handed out at the Mass, most of which had English translations alongside the Polish text. Paul Kengor first interviewed Joanne Drake about the Mass in August and September 2012, and he did so again in August 2015, via direct conversation at the Reagan Library and also via email correspondence.

6   Paul Kengor, interview with Frank Shakespeare, February 21, 2013.

7   Reagan, letter announcing he has Alzheimer's disease, Novermber 5, 1994, https://www. reaganlibrary.gov/sreference/reagan-s-letter-announcing-his-alzheimer-s-diagnosis.

8   Nick Pisa, "Vatican Hid Pope's Parkinson's Disease Diagnosis for 12 Years," *The Telegraph*, March 19, 2006, https://www.telegraph.co.uk/news/worldnews/europe/italy/1513421/ Vatican-hid-Popes-Parkinsons-disease-diagnosis-for-12-years.html.

ACKNOWLEDGMENTS

T his book would not have been possible without the material provided by the extraordinary cast who agreed to be interviewed for Robert Orlando's documentary film *The Divine Plan*: Richard V. Allen, Anne Applebaum, Bishop Robert Barron, H.W. Brands, Douglas Brinkley, Marek Jan Chodakiewicz, Cardinal Timothy Dolan, Monika Jablonska, Stephen Kotkin, John O'Sullivan, James Rosebush, Craig Shirley, and George Weigel.

That film drew inspiration from Paul Kengor's book *A Pope and a President: John Paul II, Ronald Reagan, and the Extraordinary Untold Story of the 20th Century* (ISI Books, 2017). As the film neared completion, we realized that the more than fifty hours of interviews contained a treasure trove of insights that could not be fully captured in the documentary. We wrote this book to go not so much with the film but beyond it.

We are grateful to the wonderful work of the crew at ISI Books: Jed Donahue, the world's best editor, and Anthony Sacramone, the world's best copy editor, plus Tom Cusmano, Charlie Copeland, and others. Our thanks as well to the generous ISI supporters who helped make this book possible, including Bill and Anne Burleigh, Robert W. Ellis, and Thomas J. Posatko.

We also thank Grove City College students Erin McLaughlin, Caroline Lindey, and Mitchell Kengor for their input.

From Robert Orlando

As a filmmaker, first and foremost, I am driven by questions that remain unanswered. My films are a way of exploring those answers, as I do my own research and interviews to find the true story. After years at this, I've found that there is always more to a story than just the story. I aim to bring to light what lies below the surface. Searching for the human perspective, I try to put myself in the characters' shoes to understand motivations and what effect the characters have on the world. My job is to offer, as Hamlet says of the players, the "abstract and brief chronicles of the time."

But first comes the personal story. I was immediately intrigued when I read Paul Kengor's vivid and convincing book *A Pope and a President*. Epic in scale, it told me things I had never known and made me yearn to know more. I had a substantial knowledge of Ronald Reagan and a foundational understanding of John Paul II, but suddenly I wanted to find the people behind the public performers—the ever-smiling president and the pope resplendent in his papal robes. And I was willing to have my preconceptions shattered as I went on the journey that became the film (and book).

During the filmmaking, I became the obsessed detective, trying to answer all the questions—trivial and profound—that haunted me about these two men. I read incessantly. I chased after all the talking heads in the film. And what an extraordinary and enlightening experience it was to talk with them. How to understand these two seemingly simple men with their gentle touch who so well grasped the uses of power and influence? And who were able to do so with a touch of grace and, as Marek Jan Chodakiewicz says in the film, about John Paul II, with "love."

The more I learned about John Paul II, the more I came to understand him, above all, as a Christian humanist, which connected him with other human beings—of the Church and beyond. His dignity, his spirituality, his sense of inclusion make up the immediate image. But I also found the savvy, political side that enabled him to understand and outmaneuver his Soviet enemies. He knew his God, but he wanted to know his enemy.

And Ronald Reagan? What I realized was that underneath that genial facade was a man well prepared with details of the things he needed to know (an actor's preparation), never more so than at the Reykjavik summit, when he outsmarted Gorbachev. I also learned that he really was a decent man whose innate, unshakable optimism enabled him to turn hardships into the high road.

That brings me back to one of the discoveries for the film: that Karol Wojtyła was also a superb actor. As many of our interview subjects pointed out, acting helped prepare John Paul II and Ronald Reagan for their performances on the world stage. Because of their earlier training, they knew how to stake a position and convey its complexities in simple, memorable, convincing terms like "Tear down this wall" and "Be not afraid." Of course, they were more than showmen. As H. W. Brands says in his interview, as actors they learned the importance of knowing your subject matter and knowing how to perform the role.

Reagan and John Paul II also shared a heartfelt faith, although Reagan did not always advertise his faith in public. Their faith gave them moral clarity about the horrors the Soviet regime was inflicting on Eastern Europe. They were appalled. They weren't paralyzed by nuance or compelled to make excuses for the Soviets. They knew something had to be done, and they shared the conviction that they were the ones to do it. They were men of faith, but they were also men of action. And together they changed the last part of the twentieth century.

More than anything else, I was fascinated by the bond these two seemingly dissimilar men shared. And through the making of the film, my own bond with Paul Kengor grew. His knowledge, passion, and encouragement were invaluable in the nearly year and a half I spent on the film. I can honestly call this great scholar a brother.

I also deepened my bonds with my business partner, friend, and also a brother, David Treene. David's support and continuous faith and insight allowed me the freedom to learn, experiment, and create. Without him, this film would not have been possible.

I must also thank Brian McDonald, the person willing to take the original chance on my vision that resulted in this film. Thanks, too, to my friend Ted Deutsch, the original spark, and Ila Stanger, editor par excellence, for making sense of my scribblings.

My thanks would be incomplete if I didn't mention my uncles Joseph and John Coppola, who passed on last year (2018), and my own father, Raymond Orlando, very much alive. They have been models in the art of conversation, exhibited at many a holiday table. Whenever I begin an interview, I am aware of their presence.

Lastly, thank you to my wife, Margo, who always plays her leading role in the Divine Plan with a diligence and a calm resolve that steadies the course. And my son, Dante, who has taught me so much about myself as I try to perfect my own role as father in the DP.

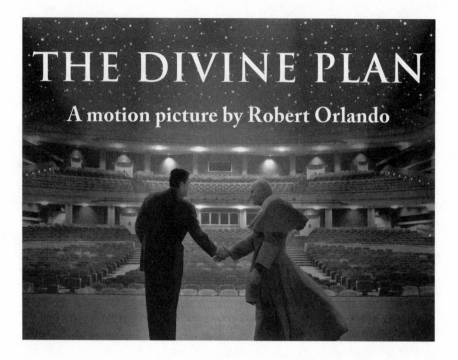

INTERCOLLEGIATE
STUDIES INSTITUTE

think. live free.™

ISI Books is the publishing imprint of the
Intercollegiate Studies Institute.

Most thoughtful college students are sick of getting a
shallow education in which too many viewpoints are
shut out and rigorous discussion is shut down.

We teach them the principles of liberty and plug them
into a vibrant intellectual community so that they
get the collegiate experience they hunger for.

www.isi.org